Ghosts and Journeys

Born in 1929, Robert Westall experienced the Blitz on Tyneside and later, between the Universities of Durham and London, acted as an unpaid lance-corporal in the Royal Signals. This experience taught him more than either university did, especially how to survive large and rigid organizations.

From 1960 until 1985, he was Head of Art and Careers at Sir John Deane's Sixth Form College, Northwich, Cheshire, where he found the heroes of his books got older as his pupils grew older.

He ran an antique shop for several years, where, being much preoccupied with the nature of time, he mainly sold clocks.

Robert Westall is now a full-time writer, and lives in Lymm, Cheshire. In 1989 he was awarded the nine-to-eleven years category Smarties Prize for *Blitzcat*.

Also by Robert Westall in Piper

Ghosts and Journeys

Short Stories

ROBERT WESTALL

Piper Books
in association with
Macmillan Children's Books

For Bridget and Loki

First published in Great Britain 1988 by
Macmillan Children's Books
This Piper edition published 1989 by Pan Books Ltd,
Cavaye Place, London SW10 9PG
in association with Macmillan
3 5 7 9 8 6 4 2
© Robert Westall 1985, 1988

ISBN 0 330 30904 8

Printed in England by Clays Ltd, St Ives plc

"The Boys' Toilets" first appeared in *Cold Feet*,
published in 1985 by Hodder & Stoughton
"Rosalie" is also available as a single story in Level 3 of the
R & D series, published by Macmillan Education 1988

Contents

The Boys' Toilets

The January term started with a scene of sheer disaster. A muddy excavator was chewing its way across the netball-court, breakfasting on the tarmac with sinuous lunges and terrifying swings of its yellow dinosaur neck. One of the stone balls had been knocked off the gateposts, and lay in crushed fragments, like a Malteser trodden on by a giant. The entrance to the science wing was blocked with a pile of ochreous clay, and curved glazed drainpipes were heaped like school dinners' macaroni.

The girls hung round in groups. One girl came back from the indoor toilets saying Miss Bowker was phoning County Hall, and using words that Liza Bottom had nearly been expelled for last term. She was greeted with snorts of disbelief....

The next girl came back from the toilet saying that Miss Bowker was nearly crying.

Which was definitely a lie, because here was Miss Bowker now, come out to address them in her best sheepskin coat. Though she *was* wearing fresh make-up, and her eyes were suspiciously bright, her

1

famous chin was up. She was brief, and to the point. There was an underground leak in the central heating; till it was mended, they would be using the old Harvest Road boys' school. They would march across now, by forms, in good order, in the charge of the prefects. She knew they would behave immaculately, and that the spirit of Spilsby Girls' Grammar would overcome all difficulties. . . .

"Take more than school spirit," said Wendy Falstaff.

"More than a bottle of whisky," said Jennifer Mount, and shuddered.

Rebeccah, who was a vicar's daughter, thought of Sodom and Gomorrah; both respectable suburbs by comparison with Harvest Road. Harvest Road was literally on the wrong side of the tracks. But obediently they marched. They passed through the streets where they lived, gay with yellow front doors, picture windows, new carports and wrought-iron gates. It was quite an adventure at first. Staff cars kept passing them, their rear windows packed with whole classrooms. Miss Rossiter, with her brass microscopes and stuffed ducks; Mademoiselle, full of tape-recorders and posters of the French wine-growing districts. Piles of the *Merchant of Venice* and "Sunflowers" by Van Gogh. . . .

The first time they passed, the teachers hooted cheerfully. But coming back they were silent, just their winkers winking, and frozen faces behind the wheel.

Then the marching columns came to a miserable little hump-backed bridge over a solitary railway-line, empty and rusting. Beyond were the same kind of houses; but afflicted by some dreadful disease, of which the symptoms were a rash of small window-panes, flaking paint, overgrown funereal privet-hedges and sagging gates that would never shut again. And then it seemed to grow colder still, as the slum-clearances started, a great empty plain of broken brick, and the wind hit them full, sandpapering faces and sending grey berets cartwheeling into the wilderness.

And there, in the midst of the desolation, like a dead sooty dinosaur, like a blackened, marooned, many-chimneyed Victorian battleship, lay Harvest Road school.

"Abandon hope, all ye who enter here," said Jennifer Mount.

"We who are about to die salute you," said Victoria.

Rebeccah thought there were some advantages to having a classical education after all.

They gathered, awed, in the hall. The windows, too high up to see out of, were stained brown round the edges; the walls were dark green. There was a carved oak board, a list of prize-winners from 1879 to 1923. Victoria peered at it. "It's BC, not AD," she announced. "The first name's Tutankhamun." There were posters sagging off the walls, on the extreme ends of long hairy strands of sticky tape; things like "Tea-Picking in India" and "The Meaning of Empire Day." It all felt rather like drowning in a very dirty goldfish-tank.

A lot of them wanted the toilet, badly. Nervousness and the walk through the cold. But nobody felt like asking till Rebeccah did. Last door at the end of the corridor and across the yard; they walked down, six strong.

They were boys' toilets. They crept past the male

3

mystery of the urinals, tall, white and rust-streaked as tombs, looking absurd, inhuman, like elderly invalid-carriages or artificial limbs. In the bottom gulley, fag-ends lay squashed and dried out, like dead flies.

And the graffiti. . . . Even Liza Bottom didn't know what some words meant. But they were huge, and hating; the whole wall screamed with them, from top to bottom. Most of the hate seemed directed at someone called "Barney Boko".

Rebeccah shuddered; that was the first shudder. But Vicky only said practically, "Bet there's no toilet-paper!" and got out her French exercise-book. . . . She was always the pessimist; but on this occasion she hadn't been pessimistic enough. Not only was there no toilet-paper, but no wooden seats, either; and the lavatory-chains had been replaced by loops of hairy thick white string, like hangman's nooses. And in the green paint of the wooden partitions the hatred of Barney Boko had been gouged half an inch deep. And the locks had been bust off all the doors except the far end one. . . .

Rebeccah, ever public-spirited and with a lesser need, stood guard stoutly without.

"Boys," she heard Victoria snort in disgust. "It's a nunnery for me. At least in nunneries they'll have soft toilet-paper."

"Don't you believe it, " said Joanne, their Roman Catholic correspondent. "They wear hair-shirts, nuns. Probably the toilets have *scrubbing-brushes* instead of paper."

Lively squeaks, all down the line, as the implications struck home.

"Some boys aren't bad," said Liza, "if you can get them away from their friends."

4

"Why bother?" said Vicky. "I'll settle for my poster of Duran Duran...."

"It's funny," said Tracy, as they were combing their hair in the solitary cracked, fly-spotted, pocket-handkerchief-sized mirror. "You know there's six of us? Well, I heard seven toilets flush. Did anybody pull the chain twice?"

They all looked at each other, and shook their heads. They looked back down the long shadowy loo, with its tiny high-up pebbled windows, towards the toilets. They shouted, wanting to know who was there, because nobody had passed them, nobody had come in.

No answer, except the sound of dripping.

The big attraction at break was the school boiler-house. They stood round on the immense coke-heaps, some new, some so old and mixed with the fallen leaves of many autumns they were hardly recognizable as coke at all. One actually had weeds growing on it....

Inside the boiler-house, in a red hissing glow, two men fought to get Harvest Road up to a reasonable temperature, somewhere above that of Dracula's crypt. One was young, cheerful, cocky, with curly brown hair; they said he was from County. The other was tall and thin, in a long grey overall-coat and cap so old the pattern had worn off. They said he was the caretaker of the old school, brought out of retirement because only he knew the ropes; he had such an expression on his face that they immediately called him Crippen. Occasionally, the cocky one would stop shovelling coke into the gaping red maw of the furnace and wipe his brow; that, and the occasional draught of warm air, immediately swept away by the biting wind, was the only hint of heat they had that morning.

The lesson after break was maths, with Miss Hogg. Miss Hogg was one of the old school: grey hair in a tight bun, tweeds, gold-rimmed spectacles. A brilliant mathematician who had once unbent far enough, at the end of the summer term, to tell the joke about the square on the hypotenuse. Feared but not loved, Miss Hogg made it quite clear to all that she had no time for men. Not so much a Female Libber as a Male Oppressor. . . .

They ground away steadily at quadratic equations, until the dreary cold, seeping out of the tiled walls into their bones, claimed Rebeccah as its first victim. Her hand shot up.

"You should have gone at break," said Miss Hogg.

"I did, Miss Hogg."

Miss Hogg's gesture gave permission, while despairing of all the fatal weaknesses of femininity.

Rebeccah hesitated just inside the doorway of the loo. The length of the low dark room, vanishing into shadow; the little green windows high up that lit nothing; the alien-ness of it all made her hesitant, as in some old dark church. The graffiti plucked at the corners of her eyes, dimly, like memorials on a church wall. But no "dearly beloveds" here.

JACKO IS A SLIMER
F— OFF HIGGINS

Where were they now? How many years ago? She told herself they must be grown men, balding with wives and families and little paunches under cardigans their wives had lovingly knitted for them. But she couldn't believe it. They were still here somewhere, fighting, snorting bubbles of blood from streaming noses, angry. Especially angry with Barney Boko. She went down the long room on tiptoe, and went into the far-end toilet because it was the only one with a lock. Snapped home the bolt so hard it echoed up and down the concrete ceiling. Only then, panting a little, did she settle. . . .

But no sooner had she settled than she heard someone come in. Not a girl; Rebeccah had quick ears. No, big boots, with steel heel-plates. Walking authoritatively towards her. From the liveliness of the feet she knew it wasn't even a man. A boy. She heard him pause, as if he sensed her; as if looking round. Then a boy's voice, quiet.

"OK, Stebbo, all clear!"

More stamping heel-capped feet tramping in. She knew she had made a terrible mistake. There must still be a boys' school here, only occupying part of the buildings. And she was in the *boys'* loo. She blushed. An enormous blush that seemed to start behind her ears, and went down her neck over her whole body. . . .

But she was a sensible child. She told herself to be calm. Just sit, quiet as a mouse, till they'd gone. She sat, breathing softly into her handkerchief, held across her mouth.

But supposing they tried the door, shouted to know who was in there? Suppose they put their hands on the top of the wooden partition and hauled themselves up and looked over the top. There were some awful *girls* who did that. . . .

But they seemed to have no interest in her locked cubicle. There was a lot of scuffling, a scraping of steel heel-plates and a panting. As if they were dragging somebody....

The somebody was dragged into the cubicle next door. Elbows thumped against the wooden partition, making her jump.

"Get his head down," ordered a sharp voice.

"No, Stebbo. *No!* Let me go, you bastards...."

"Ouch!"

"What's up?"

"Little sod bit me...."

"Get his head down, then!"

The sounds of heaving, scraping, panting, and finally a sort of high-pitched whining, got worse. Then suddenly the toilet next door flushed, the whining stopped, then resumed as a series of half-drowned gasps for breath. There was a yip of triumph, laughter, and the noise of many boots running away.

"Bastards," said a bitter, choking voice. "And you've broken my pen an' all." Then a last weary pair of boots trailed away.

She got herself ready, listening, waiting, tensed. Then undid the bolt with a rush and ran down the empty echoing place. Her own footsteps sounded frail and tiny, after the boys'. Suppose she met one, coming in?

But she didn't. And there wasn't a boy in sight in the grey high-walled yard. Bolder, she looked back at the entrance of the loo; it was the same one they'd used earlier, the one they'd been told to use. Miss Bowker must have made a mistake; someone should be told. ...

But when she got back to the classroom, and Miss

8

Hogg and all the class looked up, she lost her nerve.

"You took your time, Rebeccah," said Miss Hogg suspiciously.

"We thought you'd pulled the chain too soon and gone down to the sea-side," said Liza Bottom, playing for a vulgar laugh and getting it.

"Let me see your work so far, Liza," said Miss Hogg frostily, killing the laughter like a partridge shot on the wing.

"What's up?" whispered Vicky. "You met a fellah or something – all blushing and eyes shining. . . ." Vicky was much harder to fool than Miss Hogg.

"Tell you at lunch. . . . "

"The next girl I see talking. . . ." said Miss Hogg ominously.

But they didn't have to wait till lunch. Liza had twigged that something was up. Her hand shot up; she squirmed in her seat almost too convincingly.

"Very well, Liza. I suppose I must brace myself for an epidemic of weak bladders. . . ."

Liza returned like a bomb about to explode, her ginger hair standing out from her head like she'd back-combed it for Saturday night, a deep blush under her freckles and green eyes wide as saucers. She opened her mouth to speak – but Miss Hogg had an eagle eye for incipient hysteria, and a gift for nipping it in the bud.

"Shut the door, Liza; we'll keep the draughts we have."

Liza sat down demurely; but even the Hogg's frost couldn't stop the idea flaring across the class that something was excitingly amiss in the loos.

It was droopy Margie Trawson who blew it. She went

next; and came back and bleated, with the air of a victimized sheep that only she could achieve: "Miss, there's boys in the toilet. . . ."

"Boys?" boomed Miss Hogg. "*Boys?*" She swept out of the classroom door with all the speed her strongly muscled legs could give her. From the classroom windows they watched as she entered the toilets. Rebeccah, who was rather keen on naval warfare in the Second World War, thought she looked like an angry little frigate, just itching to depth-charge any boy out of existence. But when she emerged, her frown told that she'd been cheated of her prey. She scouted on for boys lurking behind the coke-heaps, behind the dustbins, behind the sagging fence of the caretaker's house. Nothing. She looked back towards her classroom windows, making every girlish head duck simultaneously, then headed for the Headmistress's office.

In turn, they saw the tall stately figure of the Head inspect the loo, the coke-heaps, fence and dustbins, Miss Hogg circling her on convoy-duty. But without success. Finally, after a word, they parted. Miss Hogg returned with a face like thunder.

"Someone", she announced, "has been silly. Very, *very* silly." She made *silly* sound as evil as running a concentration camp. "The Head has assured me that this school has been disused for many years, and there cannot possibly be a single boy on the premises. The only . . . males . . . are the caretakers. Now, Margie, what have you got to say to *that*? Well, Margie . . . *well*?"

There was only one end to Miss Hogg's well-Margie-well routine. Margie gruesomely dissolving into tears.

"There was boys, miss, I heard them, miss, hon-eest. . . . " She pushed back a tear with the cuff of her cardigan.

Liza was on her feet, flaming. "I heard them, too, miss." That didn't worry Miss Hogg. Liza was the form trouble-maker. But then Rebeccah was on her feet. "I heard them as well."

"*Rebeccah*. You are a clergyman's daughter. I'm ashamed of you."

"I *heard* them." Rebeccah clenched her teeth; there would be no shifting her. Miss Hogg looked thoughtful.

"They don't come when you're in a crowd, miss," bleated Margie. "They only come when you're there by yourself. They put another boy's head down the toilet an' pull the chain. They were in the place next to me."

"And to me," said Liza.

"And to me," said Rebeccah.

A sort of shiver went round the class; the humming and buzzing stopped, and it was very quiet.

"Very well," said Miss Hogg. "We will test Margie's theory. *Come,* Rebeccah!"

At the entrance to the toilet, Rebeccah suddenly felt very silly.

"Just go in and behave normally," said Miss Hogg. "I shall be just outside."

Rebeccah entered the toilet, bolted the door and sat down.

"Do exactly what you would normally do," boomed Miss Hogg suddenly, scarily, down the long dark space. Rebeccah blushed again, and did as she was told.

"There," boomed Miss Hogg, after a lengthy pause.

"Nothing, you see. Nothing at all. You girls are *ridiculous*!" Rebeccah wasn't so sure. There was something – you couldn't call it a sound – a sort of vibration in the air, like boys giggling in hiding.

"Nothing," boomed Miss Hogg again. "Come along – we've wasted enough lesson-time. Such nonsense."

Suddenly a toilet flushed at the far end of the row.

"Was that you, Rebeccah?"

"No, Miss Hogg."

"Rubbish. Of course it was."

"No, miss."

Another toilet flushed, and another, getting nearer. That convinced Miss Hogg. Rebeccah heard her stout brogues come in at a run, heard her banging back the toilet-doors, shouting: "Come out, whoever you are. You can't get away. I know you're there."

Rebeccah came out with a rush to meet her.

"Did you pull your chain Rebeccah?"

"Didn't need to, miss."

And, indeed, all the toilet doors were now open, and all the toilets manifestly empty, and every cistern busy refilling; except Rebeccah's.

"There must be a scientific explanation," said Miss Hogg. "A fault in the plumbing."

But Rebeccah thought she heard a quiver in her voice, as she stared suspiciously at the small inaccessible ventilation-grids.

They all went together at lunchtime, and nothing happened. They all went together at afternoon break, and nothing happened. Then it was time for Miss Hogg again. Black Monday was called Black Monday because they had Miss Hogg twice for maths.

And still the cold worked upon their systems. . . .

Margie Trawson again.

"Please miss, I *got* to."

Only . . . there was a secret in Margie's voice, a little gloaty secret. They all heard it; but, if Miss Hogg did, she only raised a grizzled eyebrow. "Hurry, then. If only your *mind* was so active, Margie."

She was gone a long time; a very long time. Even Miss Hogg shifted her brogued feet restlessly, as she got on with marking the other third-year form's quadratic equations.

And then Margie was standing in the doorway, and behind her the looming grey-coated figure of Crippen, with his mouth set so hard and cruel another poisoning was obviously imminent. He had Margie by the elbow in a grip that made her writhe. He whispered to Miss Hogg. . . .

"Appalling," boomed Miss Hogg. "I don't know what these children think they are coming to. Thank you for telling me so quickly, Caretaker. It won't happen again. I assure you, it won't happen again. That will be all!"

Crippen, robbed of his moment of public triumph and infant-humiliation, stalked out without another word.

"Margie," announced Miss Hogg, "has attempted to use the caretaker's outside toilet. The toilet set aside for his own personal use. A *man's* toilet. . . ."

"Obviously a hanging offence," muttered Victoria, *sotto voce,* causing a wild but limited explosion of giggles, cut off as by a knife, by Miss Hogg's glint-spectacled *look*. "How would you like it, Margie, if some strange men came into your backyard at home and used *your* toilet?"

"It'd really turn her on," muttered Victoria. Liza choked down on a giggle so hard, she nearly gave herself a slipped disc.

"No girl will ever do such a thing again," said Miss Hogg in her most dreadful voice, clutching Margie's elbow as cruelly as Crippen had. A voice so dreadful and so seldom heard that the whole form froze into thoughtfulness. Not since that joke with the chewing-gum in the first year had they heard *that* voice.

"Now, Margie, will you go and do what you have to do, in the place where you are meant to do it?"

"Don't want to go no more, miss. It's gone off . . ."

Liar, thought Rebeccah; Margie needed to go so badly she was squirming from foot to foot.

"*Go!*" said Miss Hogg, in the voice that brooked no argument. "I shall watch you from the window."

They all watched her go in; and they all watched her come out.

"Sit down quickly, Margie," said Miss Hogg. "There seems to be some difficulty with question twelve. It's quite simple really." She turned away to the blackboard, chalk in hand. "X squared, plus 2y. . . ." The chalk squeaked abominably, getting on everyone's nerves; there was a slight but growing disturbance at the back of the class, which Miss Hogg couldn't hear for the squeaking of the chalk. "3x plus 5y. . . ."

"Oh, *miss!*" wailed Margie. "I'm sorry, miss . . . I didn't mean to. . . ." Then she was flying to the classroom door, babbling and sobbing incoherently. She scrabbled for the doorknob and finally got the door open. Miss Hogg moved across swiftly and tried to grab her, but she was just too slow; Margie was gone,

14

with Miss Hogg in hot pursuit, hysterical sobs and angry shouts echoing round the whole school from the pair of them.

"What . . .?" asked Rebeccah, turning. Vicky pointed silently, at a wide spreading pool of liquid under Margie's desk.

"She never went at all," said Vicky grimly. "She must have hidden just inside the loo doorway. She was too scared. . . ."

It was then that Rebeccah began to hate the ghosts in the boys' toilets.

She tapped on Dad's study door, as soon as she got in from school. Pushed it open. He was sitting, a tall thin boyish figure, at his desk with the desk-light on. From his dejectedly drooping shoulders, and his spectacles pushed up on his forehead, she knew he was writing next Sunday's sermon. He was bashing between his eyes with a balled fist as well; Epiphany was never his favourite topic for a sermon.

"Dad?"

He came back from far away, pulled down his spectacles, blinked at her and smiled.

"It's the Person from Porlock!" This was a very ancient joke between them that only got better with time. The real Person from Porlock had interrupted the famous poet Coleridge, when he was in the middle of composing his greatest poem, 'Kubla Khan'.

"Sit down, Person," said Dad, removing a precarious tower of books from his second wooden armchair. "Want a coffee?" She glanced at his percolator; shiny and new from Mum last Christmas, but now varnished-over with dribbles, from constant use.

"Yes, please," she said, just to be matey; he made his coffee as strong as poison.

"How's Porlock?" He gave her a sharp sideways glance through his horn-rimmed spectacles. "Trouble?"

Somehow, he always knew.

She was glad she could start at the beginning, with ordinary things like the central heating and the march to Harvest Road. . . .

When she had finished, he said: "Ghosts. Ghosts in the toilet. Pulling chains and frightening people." He was the only adult she knew who wouldn't have laughed or made some stupid remark. But all he said was "Something funny happened at that school. It was closed down. A few years before Mum and I came to live here. It had an evil name; but I never knew for what."

"But what can we *do*? The girls are terrified."

"Go at lunchtime – go at break – go before you leave home."

"We do. But it's so cold. Somebody'll get caught out sooner or later."

"You won't be at Harvest Road long; even central heating leaks don't go on for ever. Shall I try to find out how long? I know the Chairman of Governors."

"Wouldn't do any harm," said Rebeccah grudgingly.

"But you don't want to wait to go that long?" It was meant to be a joke, but it died halfway between them.

"Look," said Rebeccah, "if you'd seen Margie . . . she . . . she won't dare come back. Somebody could be . . . terrified for life."

"I'll talk to your Headmistress. . . ." He reached for the phone.

"*No!*" It came out as nearly a shout. Dad put the phone back, looking puzzled. Rebeccah said, in a low voice: "The teachers think we're nuts. They'll . . . think you're nuts as well. You . . . can't afford to have people think *you're* nuts. Can you?"

"Touché," he said ruefully. "So what do you want, Person?"

"Tell me how to get rid of them. How to frighten them away, so they leave people *alone*."

"I'm not in the frightening business, Person."

"But the Church. . . ."

"You mean bell, book and candle? No can do. The Church doesn't like that kind of thing any more . . . doesn't believe in it, I suppose. . . ."

"But it's *real*." It was almost a wail.

"The only man I know who touches that sort of thing has a parish in London. He's considered a crank."

"*Tell me what to do!*"

They looked at each other in silence, a very long time. They were so much alike, with their blond hair, long faces, straight noses, spectacles. Even their hair was the same length; he wore his long, she wore hers shortish.

Finally he said: "There's no other way?"

"No."

"I don't know much. You're supposed to ask its name. It has to tell you – that's in the Bible. That's supposed to give you power over it. Then, like Shakespeare, you can ask it whether it's a spirit of health or goblin damned. Then . . . you can try commanding it to go to the place prepared for it. . . ." He jumped up, running his fingers through his hair. "No, you mustn't do any of this, Rebeccah. I can't have you doing things like this. I'll ring the Head. . . ."

"You will *not!*"

"Leave it alone, then!"

"If it lets me alone." But she had her fingers crossed.

The Head came in to address them next morning, after assembly. She braced her long elegant legs wide apart, put her hands together behind her back, rocked a little, head down, then looked at them with a smile that was a hundred per cent caring and about ninety per cent honest.

"Toilets," she said doubtfully, then with an effort, more briskly: "Toilets." She nodded gently. "I can understand you are upset about the toilets. Of all the things about this dreadful place that County's put us in, those toilets are the worst. I want you to know that I have had the strongest possible words with County, and that those toilets will be repainted and repaired by next Monday morning. I have told them that if they fail me in this I will close the school." She lowered her head in deep thought again, then looked up, more sympathetic than ever.

"You have reached an age when you are – quite rightly – beginning to be interested in boys. There *have* been boys here – they have left their mark – and I am sad they have left the worst possible kind of mark. Most boys are not like that – not like that at all, thank God. But these boys have been *gone* for over twenty years. Let me stress that. For twenty years, this building has been used to store unwanted school furniture. You may say that there are always boys everywhere – like mice, or beetles! But with all this slum-clearance around us . . . I went out yesterday actually *looking* for a boy." She looked round with a smile, expecting a laugh. She got a few titters. "The first boy I saw was a full mile away – and he was working for a butcher in the High Street." Again, she expected a laugh, and it did not come. So she went serious again. "You have been upset by the toilets – understandably. But that is no excuse for making things up, for – and I must say it – getting hysterical. Nobody else has noticed anything in these toilets. The prefects report nothing. I have watched first and second years using them quite happily. *It is just this class.* Or, rather, three excitable girls in this class. . . . " She looked round. At Liza Bottom, who blushed and wriggled. At the empty desk where Margie should have been sitting. And at Rebeccah, who stared straight back at her, as firmly as she could. "Two of those girls do not surprise me – the third girl does." Rebeccah did not flinch, which worried the Head, who was rather fond of her. So the Head finished in rather a rush. "I want you to stop acting as feather-brained females – and act instead as the sensible hard-headed young women you are going to become. This business . . . is the sort of business that gets us despised by men . . . and there are plenty of men only too ready to despise us."

The Head swept out. A sort of deadly coldness settled over the sensible young women. It hadn't happened to the prefects, or to the first-years. The Head had just proved there were ghosts, and proved they were only after people in 3A. . . .

*

It was Fiona Mowbray who bought it. It happened so swiftly, after break. They'd all gone together at break. They never realized they'd left her there, helpless with diarrhoea, and too shy to call out. She was always the shyest, Fiona. . . .

Suddenly she appeared in the doorway, interrupting the beginning of French.

"Sit down, Feeownah," said Mam'selle gently.

But Fiona just stood there, pale and stiff as a scarecrow, swaying. There were strange twists of toilet paper all round her arms. . . .

"Feeownah," said Mam'selle again with a strange panicky quiver in her voice. Fiona opened and closed her mouth to speak four times, without a single sound coming out. Then she fainted full-length, hitting the floorboards like a sack of potatoes.

Then someone ran for the Head, and everyone was crowding round, and the Head was calling "Stand back, give her air" and sending Liza for Miss Hogg's smelling salts. And Fiona coming round and starting to scream and flail out. And fainting again. And talk of sending for a doctor. . . .

Right, you sod, thought Rebeccah. That's *it*! And she slipped round the back of the clustering crowd, and nobody saw her go, for all eyes were on Fiona.

Fiona must have been in the third toilet: the toilet-roll holder was empty, and the yellow paper, swath on swath of it, covered the floor and almost buried the lavatory-bowl. It was wildly torn in places, as if Fiona had had to claw her way out of it. Had it . . . been trying to smother her? Rebeccah pulled the chain automatically. Then, with a wildly beating heart, locked herself

20

in next door, and sat down with her jaw clenched and her knickers round her knees.

It was hard to stay calm. The noise of the refilling cistern next door hid all other noises. Then, as next door dropped to a trickle, she heard another toilet being pulled. Had someone else come in, unheard? Was she wasting her time? But there'd been no footsteps. Then another toilet flushed, and another and another. Then the doors of the empty toilets began banging, over and over, so hard and savagely that she thought they must splinter.

Boom, boom, boom. Nearer and nearer.

Come on, bastard, thought Rebeccah, with the hard centre of her mind; the rest of her felt like screaming.

Then the toilet pulled over her own head. So violently it showered her with water. She looked up, and the hairy string was swinging, with no one holding it . . . like a hangman's noose. Nobody could possibly have touched it. .

The cistern-lever was pulled above her, again and again. Her nerve broke, and she rushed for the door. But the bolt wouldn't unbolt. Too stiff – too stiff for her terrified fingers. She flung herself round wildly, trying to climb over the top, but she was so terrified she couldn't manage that, either. She ended up cowering down against the door, head on her knees and hands over her ears, like an unborn baby.

Silence. Stillness. But she knew that, whatever it was, it was still there.

"What . . . is . . . your . . . name?" she whispered, from a creaky throat. Then a shout. *"What is your name?"*

As if in answer, the toilet-roll began to unroll itself,

rearing over her in swirling yellow coils, as if it wanted to smother her.

"Are you a spirit of health or goblin damned?" That reminded her of Dad, and gave her a little chip of courage. But the folds of paper went on rearing up, till all the cubicle was filled with the yellow, rustling mass. As if you had to *breathe* toilet paper.

"Begone . . . to the place . . . prepared for you," she stammered, without hope. The coils of paper moved nearer, touching her face softly.

"What do you want?" She was screaming.

There was a change. The whirling folds of paper seemed to coalesce. Into a figure, taller than herself, as tall as a very thin boy might be, wrapped in yellow bands like a mummy, with two dark gaps where eyes might have been.

If it had touched her, her mind would have splintered into a thousand pieces.

But it didn't. It just looked at her, with its hole-eyes, and swung a yellow-swathed scarecrow arm to point to the brickwork above the cistern.

Three times. Till she dumbly nodded.

Then it collapsed into a mass of paper round her feet.

After a long time, she got up and tried the doorbolt. It opened easily, and her fear changed to embarrassment as she grabbed for her pants.

It hadn't wanted to harm her at all; it had only wanted to show her something.

Emboldened, she waded back through the yellow mass. Where had it been pointing?

There could be no mistake; a tiny strand of toilet paper still clung to the brickwork, caught in a crack.

She pulled it out, and the white paintwork crumbled a little and came with it, leaving a tiny hole. She touched the part near the hole, and more paint and cement crumbled; she scrabbled, and a whole half-brick seemed to fall out into her hand. Only it wasn't all brick, but crumbly dried mud, which broke and fell in crumbs all over the yellow paper.

What a mess! But left exposed was a square black hole, and there was something stuck inside. She reached in, and lifted down a thick bundle of papers. . . .

Something made her lock the door, sit down on the toilet, and pull them out of their elastic band, which snapped with age as she touched it. Good Heavens. . . . Her mouth dropped open, appalled.

There was a dusty passport, and a wallet. The wallet was full of money, notes. Pound notes and French thousand-franc notes. And a driving-licence, made out in the name of a Mr Alfred Barnett. And letters to Mr Barnett. And tickets for trains and a cross-Channel ferry . . . and the passport, dated to expire on the first of April 1958, was also made out in the names of Alfred and Ada Barnett. . . .

She sat there, and church-child that she was, she cried a little with relief and the pity of it. The ghost was a boy who had stolen and hidden the loot, so well concealed, all those years ago. And after he was dead, he was sorry, and wanted to make amends. But the school was abandoned by then; no one to listen to him; old Crippen would never listen to a poor lost ghost. . . . Well, she would make amends for him, and then he would be at rest, poor lonely thing.

She looked at the address in the passport. "Briardene", Millbrook Gardens, Spilsby. Why, it was only ten minutes' walk; she could do it on her way home tonight, and they wouldn't even worry about her getting home a bit late.

She was still sitting there in a happy and pious daze at the virtue of the universe, when faithful Vicky came looking for her. Only faithful Vicky had noticed she was gone. So she told her, and Vicky said she would come as well....

"They've taken Fiona to hospital...."

Perhaps that should have been a warning; but Rebeccah was too happy. "She'll get over it; and once we've taken this, it won't hurt anybody else again."

It all seemed so simple.

Liza came, too, out of sheer nosiness, but Rebeccah was feeling charitable to all the world. It was that kind of blessed evening you sometimes get in January, lovely and bright, that makes you think of spring before the next snow falls.

Millbrook Gardens was in an older, solider district than their own; posher in its funny old way. Walls of brick that glowed a deep rich red in the setting sun, and showed their walking blue girlish shadows, where there wasn't any ivy or the bare strands of Virginia creeper. So it seemed that dim ghosts walked with them, among the houses with their white iron conservatories and old trees with home-made swings, and garden-seats still damp from winter. And funny stuffy names like "Lynfield" and "Spring Lodge" and "Nevsky Villa". It was hard to find "Briardene" because there were no numbers on the houses. But they found it at last, looked over the gate and saw a snowy-haired,

24

rosy-cheeked old man turning over the rose-beds in the big front garden.

He was quite a way from the gate; but he turned and looked at them. It wasn't a nice look; a long examining unfriendly look. They felt he didn't like children; they felt he would have liked to stop them coming in. But when Rebeccah called, in a too-shrill voice, "Do the Barnetts live here?" he abruptly waved them through to the front door, and went back to his digging. Rebeccah thought he must be the gardener; his clothes were quite old and shabby.

They trooped up to the front door and rang. There was no answer for quite a long time, then the image of a plump white-haired woman swam up the dark hall, all broken up by the stained glass in the door.

She looked a bit friendlier than the gardener, but not much; full of an ancient suspicion and wariness.

"Yes, children?" she said, in an old-fashioned bossy way.

Rebeccah held out her dusty package proudly. "We found this, I think it's yours. . . ."

The woman took it from her briskly enough; the way you take a parcel off a postman. But when she began to take off Rebeccah's new elastic band she suddenly looked so . . . as if she'd like to drop the packet and slam the door.

"It's a passport and money and tickets and things," said Rebeccah helpfully.

The woman put a hand to her eyes, to shield them as if the sunlight was too strong; she nearly fell, leaning against the door-post just in time. "Alfred," she called, "Alfred!" to the man in the garden. Then Rebeccah knew the man was her husband, and she thought the cry was almost a call for help. As if they'd been attacking the woman. . . .

The old man came hurrying up, full of petty anger at being disturbed. Until his wife handed him the packet. Then he, too, seemed to shrink, shrivel. The healthy high colour fled his cheeks, leaving only a pattern of bright broken veins, as if they'd been drawn on wrinkled fish-skin with a red Biro.

"They're . . . " said the woman.

"Yes," said the man. Then he turned on the girls so fiercely that they nearly ran away. His eyes were little and black and so full of hate that they, who had never been hit in their lives, grew afraid of being hit.

"Where did you get these?" There was authority in the voice, an ancient cruel utter authority. . . .

"At Harvest Road School. . . . I found them in the boys' toilets . . . hidden behind a whitewashed brick. . . ."

"Which toilet?" The old man had grabbed Rebeccah with a terrible strength, by the shoulders; his fingers were savage. He began to shake her.

"Eh, watch it," said Liza aggressively. "There's a law against that kind of thing."

"I think we'll go now," said Vicky frostily.

"Which toilet?"

"The far-end one," Rebeccah managed to gasp out. Staring into the old man's hot mad eyes, she was really frightened. This was not the way she'd meant things to go at all.

"How did you find it?" And: "What were *you* doing there?"

"We're using the school . . . till ours is mended . . . we have to use the boys' toilets. . . ."

"*Who* showed you?" Under his eyes, Rebeccah thought she was starting to fall to bits. Was he a lost member of the Gestapo, the Waffen SS? So she cried out, which she hadn't meant to,

"A *ghost* showed me – the ghost of a boy. It pointed to it. . . ."

"That's right," said Liza, "there *was* a ghost." Stubbornly, loyally.

It worked; another terrible change came over the old man. All the cruel strength flowed out of his fingers. His face went whiter than ever. He staggered, and clutched at the window-sill to support himself. He began to breathe in a rather terrifying loud unnatural way.

"Help me get him in," cried the woman. "Help me get him in quick."

Heaving and straining and panting and slithering on the dark polished floor, they got him through the hall and into a chintz armchair by the fire. He seemed to go unconscious. The woman went out, and came back with a tablet that she slipped into his mouth. He managed to swallow it. At first his breathing did not alter; then slowly it became more normal.

The woman seemed to come to herself; become aware of the little crowd, watching wide-eyed and gape-mouthed what they knew was a struggle between life and death.

"He'll be all right now," she said doubtfully. "You'd better be off home children, before your mothers start to worry." At the door she said: "Thank you for bringing the things, I'm sure you thought you were doing your best." She did not sound at all thankful really.

"We thought you'd better have them," said Rebeccah politely. "Even though they were so old. . . ."

The woman looked sharply at her, as she heard the question in her voice. "I suppose you'll want to tell your Headmistress what happened? You should have handed in the stuff to her, really. Well, Mr Barnett was the last Headmaster of Harvest Road – when it was boys, I mean – a secondary modern. It happened – those things were stolen on the last day of the summer term. We were going on holiday in France next day; we never went, we couldn't. My husband knew the boy who had stolen them, but he couldn't prove it. He had the school searched from top to bottom; the boy would admit nothing. It broke my husband's health. He resigned soon after, when the school had to close. Good night, children. Thank you."

She went as if to close the door on them, but Liza said sharply: "Did the boys call your husband Barney Boko?"

The woman gave a slight but distinct shudder, though it could have been the cold January evening. "Yes . . . they were cruel days, those, cruel."

Then she closed the door quickly, leaving them standing there.

They hadn't gone fifty yards when Liza stopped them, grabbing each of them frantically by the arm, as if she was having a fit or something.

"Don't have it here," said Vicky sharply. "Wait till we get you to the hospital!"

But Liza didn't laugh. "I remember now," she said.

"Listen. My dad went to that school; it was a terrible

28

place. Barney Boko – Dad said he caned the kids for everything, even for spelling mistakes. The kids really hated him; some parents tried to go to the governors an' the council, but it didn't do them any good. There was a boy called Stebbing – Barney Boko caned him once too often – he was found dead. I think it might have been in them toilets. The verdict was he fell; he had one of those thin skulls or something. They said he fell and banged his head."

They stared at each other in horror.

"Do you think Stebbing's . . . what's in the toilets now?" asked Vicky.

They glanced round the empty streets; the lovely sun had vanished, and it had got dark awfully suddenly. There was a sudden rush coming at them round the corner – a ghostly rustling rush – but it was only long-dead autumn leaves, driven by the wind.

"Yes," said Rebeccah, as calmly as she could. "I think it was Stebbing. But he hasn't got anything against *us* – we did what he wanted."

"What *did* he want?" asked Vicky.

"For me to take back what he'd stolen – to make up for the wrong he did."

"You're too good for this world, Rebeccah!"

"What do you mean?"

"Did Stebbing *feel* like he was sorry?" asked Vicky. "Making Margie wet herself? Frightening Fiona into a fit? What he did to *you*?"

Rebeccah shuddered. "He was angry. . . . "

"What we have just seen", said Vicky, "is Stebbing's revenge. . . ."

"How horrible. I don't believe that – it's too horrible. . . ."

29

"He used you, ducky. Boys will, if you let them."
Vicky sounded suddenly bitter.

"Oh, I'm not going to listen. I'm going home."

They parted in a bad silent mood with each other, though they stayed together as long as they could, through the windy streets, where the pools of light from the street-lights swayed. Rebeccah had the worst journey. She took her usual short-cut through the churchyard; before she realized what she'd done, she was halfway across and there was no point in turning back. She stood paralysed, staring at the teethlike ranks of the tombstones that grinned at her in the faintest light of the last street-lamp.

Somewhere among them, Stebbing must be buried. And the worst of it was, the oldest, Victorian gravestones were behind her, and the newer ones in front. She could just make out the date on the nearest white one.

1956.

Stebbing must be very close.

She whimpered. Then she thought of God, whom she really believed in. God wouldn't let Stebbing hurt her. She sort of reached out in her mind, to make sure God was there. In the windy night, He seemed very far away; but He *was* watching. Whimpering softly to herself, she walked on, trying not to look at the names on the tombstones, but not able to stop herself.

Stebbing was right by the path, third from the edge.

TO THE BELOVED MEMORY OF
BARRY STEBBING
BORN 11 MARCH 1944
DIED 22 JULY 1957
WITH GOD, WHICH IS MUCH BETTER

But Stebbing had nothing to say to her, here. Except perhaps, a feeling it was all over, and his quarrel had never been with her. Really.

And then she was running, and the lights of home were in front of her, and Stebbing far behind.

She burst into the front hall like a hurricane. Daddy always kept the outside front door open, and a welcoming light glowing through the inner one, even in the middle of winter.

Daddy was standing by the hallstand, looking at her. Wearing his dark grey overcoat, and carrying a little bag like a doctor's. Instinctively, as the child of the vicarage, she knew he was going to somebody who was dying.

"Oh," she said. "I wanted to talk to you." All breathless.

He smiled, but from far away; as God had. He always seemed far away when he was going to somebody who was dying.

"You'll have to wait, Person, I'm afraid. But I expect I'll be home for tea. And all the evening. The Church Aid meeting's been cancelled."

"Oh *good*." Toast made at the fire, and Daddy, and a long warm evening with the curtains drawn against the dark. . . .

"I wonder," he said vaguely, "can you help? Is Millbrook Gardens the second or third turning off Windsor Road? I can never remember. . . ."

"Second from the bottom." Then, in a rush, "Who's dying?"

He smiled, puzzled. They never talked about such things. "Just an old man called Barnett . . . heart giving out. But his wife says he's very troubled . . . wants to talk about something he did years ago that's on his mind. I'd better be off, Rebeccah. See you soon." He went out. She heard his footsteps fading down the path.

She clutched the hallstand desperately, her eyes screwed tight shut, so she wouldn't see her face in the mirror.

"Come home soon, Daddy," she prayed. "Come home soon."

The Bus

Every lunchtime, Jack queued at the bus station and watched the young mums undermining Britain.

There was one at it now.

"Dar-ren! Don't do that, Dar-ren! Come here or I'll *smack* you, Dar-ren!"

Jack eyed her. She stood in an S-shape, her pregnancy accentuated by two bulging carrier-bags, one in each hand. Her face was pale and shiny, and strands of hair, the faded brown of an old woman's, were clinging to her forehead. Yet she couldn't have been more than about twenty-three. Had she ever worn tight jeans, giggled and rocked around the clock? Impossible to believe; as it was impossible to believe that any bloke could have fancied her enough to get her in the family way again. . . .

And feeble with it. If Jack had been a betting man, he'd have put the odds against the evil Darren ever getting smacked at fifty to one.

"*Dar-ren!* Oh, do come and behave, Darren!"

Darren, aged three, continued to swing on the metal crush-barrier, within inches of the wheels of passing

33

buses. While his mum's voice bleated on and on. Jack's palms itched to grab him by the scruff of the neck and return him to the bosom of his parent. But it never worked; he'd tried it, and they didn't even thank you. Just glared at you, like you were a child molester. Maybe a passing bus, coming too close, would provide a final solution to the Darren crisis. . . .

Sensing the ill-will, the child turned and stared at Jack. Jack recognized the thick sulky pouting lips, the cunning sly look from under lowered brows, from his own days as a prefect. Larry Deakin of 4D, and a hundred other educational terrorists of short-lived fame. The sort that hung around you endlessly while you were on playground duty, muttering endless filth. But if you so much as grabbed them by the lapels they'd have their parents on to you, the school governors, even the police. And the Head wouldn't back you up in public, though he sympathized in private. Even the police sympathized in private, saying they'd like to thump the little buggers, too, but it was more than their jobs were worth. . . .

This was how the Larry Deakins of this world were made; this was how they learnt that authority could be flouted with impunity. The lesson was learnt by three years old. After that, they were simply gathering their weapons, such as flying pickets or Kalashnikov rifles; then they could go on raising hell for other people till the day they died.

Thank God my dad wasn't like this mum. Dad was a two-warning man. After two warnings, you lost the chance to watch 'Kojak', or half your week's pocket-money, or a thump landed on your ear. Dad always did what he said, and you could howl, sulk, plead or wheedle till the cows came home; you wouldn't shift him one inch. So you knew where you were with him – on solid ground. Only, as Dad said, the world didn't always give two warnings. Sometimes you got one, like before they sacked you at work. Sometimes you got none, like when you rode your motorbike on to a patch of black ice in the dark. . . .

And of course, years later, it was Larry Deakin who tampered with the brakes of Jack's bike in the works bike-shed. Just for a bit of fun, of course. Jack had escaped the front wheels of a bus by inches. He had nearly punched Larry Deakin's teeth down his throat. And when Larry's mum had gone to the police Jack had told the police about the brakes. The police had asked Jack whether he'd like to charge Larry with attempted murder. Whereupon Larry's mum had turned white and shut up, thank God.

But Jack didn't ride his bike to work any more. Which was why he was stood here, waiting for the bus. . . .

"Dar-ren! Come *here*, Dar-ren! Dar-ren, I'll *smack* you!"

Darren went on swinging.

The bus service back to the works after the lunch-hour was a bit dicey. Sometimes you got to the bus station at quarter to one, and no bus came, and you were late and got a wigging from the foreman. Other days you got to the bus station at five to one, caught a bus just going out and were back on time. There were four different buses you could catch. But it wasn't a matter of timetables; it was a matter of drivers. They ran the buses pretty much for their own convenience, and herded the waiting public round like sheep. They always made a bit of a drama out of arriving with an empty bus. First, they'd slam the hydraulic doors shut in the public's face; then they'd sit there and do a variety of things, like counting their takings, or taking off and putting on their ticket-machines, or even, if they were among the younger ones, combing their hair in the driving mirror. Then they'd cause a bit of a stir among the waiting sheep by standing up and turning a little handle in the ceiling of their cab. Everyone rushed round to the front of the bus to see where it was going. Such wildly different destinations came up; places nearly a hundred miles apart. One guy, having wound his destination-indicator backwards and forwards several times, getting all the girls agog, had finished up with his sign saying 'Private' and driven off without letting anybody aboard at all. He'd thought that a great laugh; Jack had stuck up two fingers at his departing tail-lights, but the sheep just went on standing in their queue apathetically. . . .

At this point Jack was jerked out of his angry memories by a single-decker coming in and stopping at his platform. Afterwards, he tried to remember whether there'd been anything special about it. But it was just green and marked 'Crosville' like all the others. The only difference was that when they all ran round to look at the front the destination-sign was totally blank. And the driver didn't fiddle with anything; just sat there motionless. Only, after a bit, he pressed his button inside and the doors opened with their usual hiss and swish.

Immediately, all the old biddies with their shopping trolleys and arthritic husbands began clustering round the foot of the bus-steps like eager worshippers round a shrine. They asked the usual daft questions that Jack never tired of hearing.

"Are you the Leftwich Estate, love?"

"Are you the Davenham Circular?" Since the driver was tall and very thin, Jack particularly liked that one. There was one enormously fat driver whom he always thought of as the Davenham Circular.

"Are you Winsford and Salterswall?" They made it sound like a cross-talk comedy act, like Morecambe and Wise.

"Are you the Bull's Head?" This was a new one on Jack. He had to bottle up his laugh so much he got a pain in his side.

But to all these beseechings the tall thin driver merely shook his head and went on sitting. The old biddies fell back confused and complaining about the past sins of the bus company.

But in their place came a hustling queue of strangers. Again, Jack tried to remember afterwards if there was anything different about them. But apart from few being very young, and the older ones being older than usual, Jack could remember nothing. They ascended the steps and began handing over their money.

Jack said to one of the younger ones in the queue: "Think it's wise getting on to an unmarked bus, mate? Could be going anywhere. . . ." Mainly he said it for a joke; but he was also just a little bit nosy. But the lad just stared at him, and went on up the bus-steps. Unfriendly sod; no sense of humour. Jack watched him hand over his money. And blinked.

Because Jack could have sworn he handed over just two pennies.

God, you couldn't go *anywhere* for twopence today. Minimum fare was seventeen pence for two stops. He must be seeing things.

But the next person, an old biddy, also handed over two pennies. And the next, a tall middle-aged man with a pain-wrinkled face, a heavy moustache and two sticks.

They all handed over just twopence.

A terrible curiosity seized Jack – a curiosity that had got him into trouble often. Without a thought of getting back to work, he joined the queue and shuffled forward with the rest.

He studied the driver with interest. The driver had his head down, just taking two pennies from every hand that passed. He looked pretty average for a Crosville driver: black strandy hair plastered over a bald patch with plenty of hair-cream. His cheap grey nylon jacket, with its Crosville badge on the breast was a bit too small for him; it bulged over his little bus-driver's paunch, and the sleeves pulled back up his arms exposing hairy wrists.

But when Jack held out two pennies the driver looked up. Jack was ready for that; ready to brazen it out. There were plenty of times when a hard straight stare, followed up by a cheerful grin, worked wonders; especially with women. . . .

This time it didn't work. The driver's stare was a lot harder; a pale cool green hardness that would not bend. No grin, either.

For a long moment, their stares remained locked. Then, just as Jack's was beginning to fade and drop, he had a brainwave. He held out his pennies more insistently and said, with a voice that knew its rights: "Legal fare, innit?"

It worked. The driver shrugged, looked down and took the money. Jack went on into the bus. Every seat but one was full; everyone looked at Jack with that curious lack of interest you see in bus passengers; that long slow enduring patience that has missed many a five-past-nine and had to hang on for the half-past. It was just that this lot seemed even greyer, wearier, drearier than usual. Jack took the vacant seat, just behind the driver, next to the kid he'd tried to make the joke to.

He wished he hadn't. The kid stank. More than that, he was appallingly thin. Not healthy-thin, like most kids; more like a skeleton under his greasy jeans and filthy T-shirt and smelly bomber-jacket. And there was horrible oozing yellow acne crawling up his neck from under his collar and across his cheek. And he kept shivering, and running his hands across each other, even though the bus was quite warm. And he kept sniffing, sniff, sniff, sniff, as automatically as if he was a creaky part of the bus, as the bus started up and swept out of the bus-station.

The kid still didn't make any attempt to talk, and now Jack was glad of it. He'd have moved his seat if he could; but there was no other seat. All the same, he sat as far away as possible, not wanting to touch the filth of the kid's jacket or feel the bones he sensed beneath it. Instead, he stared out of the window, past the kid's profile. No point in going on a magical mystery tour if you couldn't see where you were going.

The first odd thing he noticed was nice, so its oddness didn't strike him. They went through Tatfield Corner. There had been a smallholding there as long as Jack could remember. About five acres, surrounded by a hawthorn hedge, with a little house in the middle.

Rows and rows of cabbages and lettuces; chickens roaming free and a few goats tethered. Children riding round and round on bikes like mad things, and a woman hanging out washing sometimes.

Then, last summer, it was as if some terrible disease had hit the place. Fewer and fewer things were growing; patches of bare earth spread; till a blanket of weeds, thin as green mist at first, then thick as a devouring fog, spread over the land. The goats vanished; then the chickens. Then he didn't see the kids or the woman any more. And, though the windows of the house still had curtains up, some windows got broken. Finally, slates began to slip, leaving gaping black holes in the roof. Behind the house, yellow Portakabins appeared, with a builder's name in big black letters. Then thin lines of trenches, outlining the plan of a small factory, which a huge signboard announced was going to produce "Polyware", whatever "Polyware" was. . . .

Now, with a jerk, Jack realized the chimney of the house was smoking again. Somebody had mended the roof. There was washing on the line, and squares of good red tilled earth were driving back the weeds. And of the yellow Portakabins there was no sign.

They're back, thought Jack happily. Or somebody else, anyway. The place was going to produce living things again, not Polyware. It seemed a good omen; Jack settled back more comfortably into his seat.

And then they were running down into Pagbury, through the industrial estate which had mostly closed down in 1979 and been an empty ghost ever since. Or so he'd heard; because nobody went to Pagbury who didn't have to. Massive unemployment, everybody living off the Giro, graffiti, vandalism and . . . well, you just didn't go near Pagbury any more, that's all.

But he was surprised to see how many of the factories were working. More than half, if you judged by their wire-meshed carparks full of cars. Oh, well, you couldn't believe everything you heard....

As they ran on down the steep hill, towards the town centre, the kid sitting beside him turned and said something. Which Jack didn't hear because the kid's breath hit him like a foul gas.

But Jack didn't want to seem rude, so he said: "Yewhat?"

"Getting off here," said the kid. "Good place, this. No hard drugs; no pushers." He grasped the upright bar, ready to pull himself to his feet. He hardly seemed to have the strength to walk.

"What – *Pagbury*?" gasped Jack in amazement. Pagbury was famous for its drugs and pushers.

"No, not Pagbury," gasped the kid. "Nineteen seventy-eight I mean."

The bus drew to a halt; his hand tightened on the bar. As he hauled himself upright, his unbuttoned sleeve fell back, revealing on the inside of his thin arm a row of punctures going septic in nasty green blisters. Then, with a last whiff of foul breath, he was up and off the bus.

The hydraulic doors hissed and slammed behind him. Jack stretched with relief and moved into the window-seat. He saw the kid running, or trying to run, across the broken brick of a demolition-site, until he vanished into a thin haze that might have been mist or rain coming.

1978? What the hell had the kid meant? Was it some kind of map-reference? Or the number of the bus-stop?

Or was he just another junkie, living in a world of his own?

His eyes roved round, as if Pagbury in the rain would give him some sort of answer. But there was only a newsagent's shop, next to the demolition-site. With posters outside, in crude lettering. The one headed "Daily Mirror" announced in huge screaming letters: "POPE DIES".

Jack felt a slight stab of grief. He wasn't a Catholic, of course; he wasn't at all religious. But he'd liked the Pope, the way he went belting round the world and belted hell out of the commies. And when the Pope came to Britain Jack had got a lot of laughs at school by imitating the Pope's English.

"We must laff God, because He first laffed us..."

Jack had liked the idea of laughing God; so had all the other kids in school.

So he'd been fond of the Pope; he'd miss him. And he wasn't *old*, as Popes went. Anyway, it didn't have to be *the* Pope who'd died. Could be some bloke *called* Pope; like Dudley Pope, the bloke who wrote sea-stories. Those newsagents' billboards were full of tricks to make you buy a paper. Like when they put "FAMOUS UNITED FOOTBALLER DIES". And when you'd been fool enough to buy a paper you found it was some old gaffer who'd played for them in the 1920s, who you'd never even *heard* of.

Jack settled back in his seat again, as the bus moved off

They trundled on towards Melpam. Jack kept staring at the countryside, wondering why it looked different. There was something missing. The roadsides looked so bare and dull. It was a long time before he twigged. There were no wild flowers on the grass verges; no brilliant carpet of yellow dandelions, with a foaming mass of cow-parsley above. Great God, they'd been *mowing* the grass verges; treating them with weedkiller. In this era of Thatcherism, Melpam District Council must have money to *burn*. . . .

Then the bus-seat thumped beneath his bottom as somebody sat down next to him. He turned abruptly, frightened it might be somebody as horrible as the junkie.

But it was a little respectable old man with white hair, a cap set jauntily on top of it, and a green woolly waistcoat inside his unbuttoned coat.

The man nodded to Jack, nearly touched his cap. "How do, sir?" he said. "Not a bad morning to be startin' a new job!"

"You got a new *job*?" gasped Jack. "How *old* are you?" Then he could have bitten his lip at being so rude. But the old gaffer didn't seem to mind. He was too brimming with glee.

"Sixty-three next birthday, sir! But there's life in the old dog yet! It's only sweeping up, and cleaning out the toilets, but it's a job. I've been on the dole for eight years, so it'll be a grand change; get me out from under t' wife's feet, and money will come in handy. . ."

"Where you got the job?"

"Timmington's."

"But Timmington's closed ten years ago; they couldn't compete with Volvo and Scania . . ."

"Not what I heard," said the old man sharply. "I hear they're selling every lorry they can make." But there was a strange dishonest flicker at the back of his eyes

43

that made Jack look away from him suddenly. Was everyone on this bus a nutter? Jack stared out of the window fixedly, till the long grey shape of the derelict Timmington's came into view.

And the gates weren't chained shut; nor was there grass growing beneath them. There was even a man on duty in the gate-office, smoking a fag and supping from a mug of tea. In a dream, Jack watched the old man get off and show the man at the gate some kind of letter, and be let through.

The bus-doors hissed and slammed again. The bus jerked into heavy dieseled life, and more countryside swept past Jack's fuddled eyes.

Including an elm – in full leaf. Jack gaped, then told himself it must be one of those pampered pets of elms, shot full every year with expensive injections of chemicals to keep Dutch elm disease at bay. There were still some of those about.

But seven more living elms swept past him. Then two more. Nobody could afford to keep that many elms alive. Not even the barmy Melpam District Council.

And fixed to the base of the last elm, outside the village shop, was another newspaper advertising board. This one read: "UNEMPLOYMENT TOPS 1,000,000."

And Jack suddenly knew what sort of bus he was on.

Or he thought he did.

He must be dreaming, of course. Buses of this sort simply didn't exist. But it was quite the most interesting kind of dream, and he was determined to make the most of it before he woke up. He watched out of the window intently.

The light outside the window was dim, even when the sun appeared to be shining. And not only dim, but flickering. That would be day and night, of course. When you passed a year in a few minutes, day and night would show as a flicker. And that explained the enormous changes in the landscape. There'd be snow on the fields one minute, and brilliant sunshine the next. Not that you couldn't get that, sometimes, in April. But not trees in full leaf and gardens full of flowers as well. . . .

South of Melpam, the bus piddled along as it approached the Potteries. It was nowhere sort of country – lots of fields, but also lots of pylons, and every so often the belching chimneys of a works. And all the time it seemed to Jack there were fewer pylons, and fewer telly-aerials on the houses, and more belching chimneys. And the road was so irritatingly narrow, and full of kinky little bends. This surely wasn't any kind of *main* road?

People kept getting off. But others, obviously frightened of missing their stop, came and sat next to Jack, to be handy for when the bus-doors opened.

The first to perch beside him was a woman in a long loose raincoat and horn-rimmed glasses. Her dark hair was cut, and you couldn't say more for it than that. She had a dull skin with large pores, and as she looked at Jack her eyes moved like dark goldfish behind her glasses. Sharp and spiteful goldfish; more like miniature sharks, really.

"I shall be glad to get back," she said. Though she sounded more vicious than glad.

"Back where?"

"Back to where there's some *respect*. And . . . standards. Back to where the world was a decent place to live in."

Jack looked to the front; he knew her sort. But she wouldn't leave him alone.

"Like that," she said, pointing out of the window, across Jack's face.

And, in spite of himself, Jack looked.

The bus had stopped at traffic-lights outside a school. Behind high railings with spiked tops, ranks of children stood motionless in the playground. Absolutely motionless, like the Brigade of Guards being inspected by the Queen. Only the girls' pigtail-ribbons fluttered in the breeze; and their short skirts. Then a teacher at the top of the school steps flicked his hand, and the first double-rank filed humbly, silently and respectfully up the steps and into school.

"*That's* what I mean," said the woman. "*Respect.* Respect for teachers; respect for parents; respect for any grown-up. No lip. No answering back."

Jack didn't trust himself to say anything; just stared fixedly in front of him. But the woman had by no means finished with him.

"And look at *that!*"

In spite of himself, Jack looked again. At a perfectly normal row of terrace houses.

"What's there to look at?"

"Exactly," said the woman. "No graffiti. No 'Stoke City Rules OK'. No vandalism. No gates off their hinges. No litter. And a bus-shelter with no broken windows."

"H'm," said Jack. Actually, he was slightly impressed.

He didn't like graffiti and vandalism and litter much himself. Maybe the woman had something.

Just then the bus stopped, and the doors hissed open. He heard a woman standing at the bus-stop say: "Do that once more, Barry, and I'll *smack* you!" And almost immediately there was a loud smack and an infant wail.

"Parents meant what they said in those days," said the woman, as the bus-doors closed again. "Mind you, our dad didn't have to *hit* us – one *look* was enough. And look at *that*!" Her voice was full of admiring awe, as if she'd caught sight of the Taj Mahal.

But it wasn't the Taj Mahal; though it was nearly as strange. An old-fashioned grammar-school boy, complete with striped blazer and cap and a satchel hung correctly by both straps on his back. And, in spite of the fact that he must have been at least thirteen, he wore short trousers, and his long bare legs seemed to go on for ever, till they reached his long neat grey stockings with the coloured bands round the top. His neck and the back of his head were shaved nearly bare, so his ears stuck out like jug-handles on either side of his cap.

And as he passed an elderly woman he smiled and reached up and deliberately raised his cap to her. And she smiled and bobbed slightly in return.

"Honour thy father and thy mother," said the woman viciously. "When I was a little girl, we were on a building site, throwing sand. And this old lady told us to stop it, and I gave her cheek. Which was a bad mistake, *I* can tell you, because she was a friend of our gran's and our gran told our dad and he took off his belt and gave me the buckle-end. *And* it hasn't done me any harm, either."

47

Jack opened his mouth to disagree, but she was on her feet and the bus was slowing down again. As she got off, she gave Jack a lingering glance, as if she expected *him* to raise his nonexistent cap to her.

As the bus pulled away, they passed a cinema. Huge posters over the entrance announced Elvis Presley in his latest hit *Love Me Tender*.

1957.

Jack used the cinema-hoardings a lot after that, as they drove south out of the Potteries. As a buff of old films on telly, he found them an excellent guide.

Rommel – Desert Fox. About 1952.

The Wooden Horse. 1950.

All the little town centres were full of women shopping. No men, except a few really ancient gaffers. And under-fives out with their mums. The nation was at work. Unemployment must be down to 350,000. Everyone at work in the belching factories, except a few cripples and nutters. The police all wore pointed helmets and collars done up to their neck, and they were just standing about on street-corners, pointing out the way to people or stopping traffic so old ladies could cross the road. Not that there was much traffic. Just a sprinkling of old MG sports cars, and Jowett Javelins and razor-edged Triumphs and some very small lorries. It all seemed so peaceful and orderly and safe, Jack was half-tempted to get off. Out there, people went to Northern Ireland for their holidays. Or went to Lebanon and lay sunbathing on the beach in bikinis. Ethiopia was just a far country with beautiful postage-stamps. And Britain still stood for something; a third world superpower with a bloody great navy with battleships and carriers; and one-third of the globe was still coloured red for the British Empire....

Then somebody else sat down next to him, and said, in a broad Brummie accent: "This is the stuff, eh? I can't wait to see it!"

"What's that?"

"Brum. A Brum without niggers. A Brum without Pakis. A *British* Brum. Every face a white face. I was born in Handsworth – a decent respectable place. Little houses wi' lace curtains at the window, and the privet-hedge clipped once a week. A place where a respectable married woman could go out alone at night to see her sister, and come home close to midnight an' her husband not worry. You had *real* neighbours then, who would do your washing for you if your wife was ill, an' cook you a meal when you got home fra work, an' see to the kids. There was never a friendlier place than Brum then. You could go out of an evening an' leave your front door unlocked ... "

Deeply shocked, Jack stared round wildly. This bloke could get himself locked up, going on like that. Incitement to racial disharmony....

But no one was listening. Apart from one guy dressed in black, up towards the back, they had the bus to themselves.

He took a sideways look at the racist, expecting some great hulking member of the National Front. Instead, he saw a little balding bloke with a thin moustache and rather grubby sports coat and flannels. A little bloke who looked like he wouldn't hurt a fly. Who had tears standing in the corners of his eyes.

"Aw, don't look at me like that. You haven't had to live wi' them, wi' their bloody music wailing over the garden wall so you can't sit out in summer, an' the smell of their rancid fat puttin' you off your Sunday dinner. You haven't had your daughter accosted by two great buck niggers in cowboy hats, who smashed in your face when you tried to stop them. I've had *enough*."

To Jack's horror, he started to cry. The bloke was cracking up. Jack didn't know how to cope.

But the bus solved his problem. Again it stopped and the doors hissed open, and the man was gone, running up a street where a theatre-sign was advertising the second touring company of Ivor Novello's *We'll Gather Lilacs.*

1946.

Slowly, in a stream of traffic, they passed up a Snow Hill where every face was white; then down to where the Bullring Market was only an empty bomb-site between enormously high walls.

It was only then that Jack began to worry. It must have been the bus that had kept him feeling safe for so long. So big and solid; and everyone knew that buses ended up where they'd started from; whether they went round in a circle, like the Davenham Circular, or back and forth like the Leftwich Estate.

But now Jack noticed the bus itself seemed to have changed. It seemed shorter; the aisle narrower, the seats made of real leather instead of plastic. There was a small metal plate on the bulkhead in front, marked 'Stubber' for people to stub their fags out on; with an ashtray beneath.

On the buses he travelled on, smoking was forbidden, except for the four back seats. With a penalty of £200.

And above his head rows of leather loops hung from the ceiling, for people to stand and strap hang during the rush-hour. He found the idea of a bus being that full of people unnerving. All the buses he travelled on were more than half-empty.

He was a long way from home, in time and space. A hundred miles, and forty years. He suddenly wanted to ask the driver how far he *was* going.

But instead a figure in smelly black leathers thumped down in the seat next to him. A massive figure that clanked, in a leaden sort of way. Jack could tell from the pong of oil and petrol and unwashed socks that this was no ordinary biker. It was one of those terrible pseudo-Hell's Angels from Pagbury. Who were even worse than real Hell's Angels. Because they felt they had to smash your face in to *prove* they really were Hell's Angels, and not merely the unemployed who burgled houses to pay for petrol and oil and booze.

Jack sat as still as a mouse. With this sort, even the wrong sort of wriggle could start a fight. He just sat still and prayed the creature would get off soon.

But the creature was in a mood for confidences; high as a kite on God knew what cocktail of booze and drugs.

"This is it, eh? Just the job!"

"What?" asked Jack faintly. This sort *always* took silences wrong.

"The war o' course. Chance to screw a few Jerries. I'm goin' to join the Commandos . . . best unarmed-

combat in the world . . . squeeze your eyeballs out wi'
one finger . . . smash yer windpipe wi' one hand. . . . "

Jack stared out of the window in desperation. They
were moving very slowly through countryside, and it
was trying to grow dark.

But the dark would not come. A strange pink light
was flooding into the hedgerows and the fields – an
unreal pink.

And then he looked ahead, and saw it. A whole
jagged city skyline in flames; an inferno like the old
pictures of hell that Hieronymus Bosch had painted;
under rolling clouds that were really smoke.

And the bus had slowed because it was having to
pick its way through streams of people. Women
carrying screaming babies; men with faces turned to
the ground, carrying huge white bundles of what
looked like bedclothes. Little kids too tired to walk
being dragged along and falling and being dragged to
their feet again.

And there was no one to help them.

And though all the signposts were fingerless, just
bare posts, Jack knew this must be Coventry, and the
time 1941. . . .

And still the bus crawled on. Through streets so hot
that the doors and windows of the little houses
suddenly blistered, charred and burst into flames
without warning. And all the crazy quivering hulk
sitting next to him could say was "Great! Great!
Smashing! Great!"

Until the bus stopped, in front of the burning
cathedral itself. The doors swooshed open. A great
blast of searing heat swept in. The crazed leather-clad

figure leapt down the stairs and ran off into the heart of the flames, capering and dancing with glee at the destruction around him.

And was not consumed; but only vanished round a white-hot corner, out of sight.

It was then that Jack knew what kind of bus he was really on.

And who the passengers had been.

The bus drove on, out of Coventry and into the quiet countryside. Already the signposts were back, and the shop-windows all lit up, and people were doing their late-night shopping.

1938. Or 1937. Or 1936....

Jack saw no reason why the bus should ever stop. But in the end it did, in the darkened carpark of some roadhouse strung with coloured lights, from which a not-very-good dance-band played, and a woman singer sang through a bad microphone, "Let the great big world keep turning ... "

On the bus, the engine shuddered and died, and started to tick as it cooled. The driver sat motionless, just the back of a head and shoulders. Jack wondered in terror whether, if the driver did turn round, his face would be the same. Then he realized that, dimly, he could see the driver's face reflected in the dark windscreen. Just the faint shine of a forehead and nose, outlining the dim shadowy pits of eyes. He did not want to run the risk of speaking; but after a bit the silence became unbearable.

"I don't want to get off here," he called out, and his voice shook.

"You cannot get off here," said the driver. "You are still alive. Only the dead can go back. Even those who *want* to go back are beginning to die..."

"I never wanted to go back." But he remembered the 1950s when the kids had respect and adults meant what they said, and Britain still had an empire....

The driver was silent a long time. The singer's voice came again from the roadhouse. "Tiptoe, through the tulips, through the tulips..."

"No, I don't think you *really* wanted to go back. Though you thought about it. But you didn't really *want* to." He sounded as heavy and stern as a judge, handing down sentence.

"Who *are* you?" called out Jack, in even greater fright.

"The Greeks called us Charon, the ferryman across the River Styx. Why do you think the dead always had two pennies placed over their eyes? The two pennies are for the fare.... You paid me two pennies; you are in Death's Kingdom...."

"Please, I want to go home...."

"You accept your future, good or bad?"

Jack took a deep breath and said: "Yes."

At that moment, in the darkness of the road ahead, two headlights.

Another bus, going the other way. It pulled into the carpark, and manoeuvred alongside, till the two sets of doors were opposite each other.

"Hold your breath as you cross," said the driver. "The gap may seem only an inch, but it is the widest chasm in the universe. And the air of this kingdom.... Are you ready...?"

The two sets of doors hissed open, one after the

other. Jack stepped across the gap. The cold seared his lungs, his heart, his bones to the marrow. Stars whirled in a black bottomless sky. . . .

Then he was falling into another worn seat, and the dust of his impact went up his nose, making him sneeze. He heard the doors hiss shut.

Then he fell asleep; the same deadly sleep that haunts night-bomber crews once they have left the target.

The next thing he knew, he was leaning on the crush-barrier of the bus-station, and a single-decker was just pulling in, and Darren was still swinging disobediently to his left.

He shook himself, and carefully walked round to the front of the bus with the other sheep, to see where it was going.

But it was only a Davenham Circular.

The Borgia Mirror

"It's a nice bronze," said Mr Lipfriend coaxingly. "Italian ... cinquecento...."

"Perhaps," said Lady Portia. She eyed the female figure, which was rather improbably balanced on one foot and bending forward to dry the other foot with a very long and narrow towel. The bronze hair, caught up in an elaborate chignon, was falling loose becomingly. The towel, cunningly draped, highlighted rather than concealed the small ripe breasts and fold of plumpness across the belly. Men liked their soft porn more elegant in those days....

"I might almost have thought," said Mr Lipfriend dreamily, "that it was by the divine Benvenuto himself."

Lady Portia gave him an icy grey-eyed stare.

"Or a pupil," Mr Lipfriend added hastily, "a close pupil ... at least the *school* of Benvenuto...."

"Or a good nineteenth-century French forgery," said Lady Portia. Her voice had taken on the edge of a cut-throat razor.

Mr Lipfriend cringed inwardly, but tried not to show it. Lady Portia had made him; Lady Portia could break him. All the carpeted and spotlit splendours of his Kensington shop he owed to her and her friends. He needed her; but he hated her. And he couldn't resist a sly dig, to prove his independence.

"Very much to Lord Copfield's taste, I would have thought," he said with sweet courtly malice. He suddenly sensed he wasn't going to sell her the bronze.

"If he *has* any taste," said Lady Portia coolly. "He is spending this weekend with one of his female systems-analysts. Ex-Pimlico Comprehensive...."

"I'm sorry," said Mr Lipfriend with saccharine insincerity.

"I'm not sorry he's *away*. He can do what he damned well likes. But he keeps on getting his secretaries to tell me lies. And I can hear the other secretaries laughing in the background. I wish I could buy him a birthday present that would keep him at home for a bit, instead of running around making fools of both of us."

"I had something in the shop last week that would have kept him home for a bit," said Mr Lipfriend, eyes half-closed reminiscently. "A huge bedroom mirror – again Italian cinquecento. Said to have come from the palace of the Borgias. I can't imagine what that must have seen, in its time...."

Lady Portia snorted. "If you don't stop spinning your fairy-tales, Mr Lipfriend, you'll end up in court." Her eyes had grown even colder. She'd quite liked Lipfriend when he was all West End and vulgar; all velvet jackets and diamond tie-pins. Now he had a house in the country he had taken to wearing tweeds, especially on Saturday mornings; the effect was revolting.

"A sixteenth-century mirror, I *swear*," said Mr Lipfriend with a refreshing return to West End vulgarity. "All of five feet tall. Cherubs. Gilt all worn away. Steel mirror. The real stuff."

In spite of the Borgia nonsense, Lady Portia's appetite was aroused. Fine old things had become her whole life since Lord Copfield had taken to going the rounds of his female employees. "What happened to it?"

"We're shipping it to the States."

"Without an export licence?" asked Lady Portia, going in for the kill.

Mr Lipfriend flinched again. Lady Portia followed up her advantage.

"I'll see it. Where is it?"

There was a lot of umming and ahing. Mr Lipfriend had to ring up two associates and use all his powers of persuasion. Finally, he wrote an address on a sheet of his exquisite notepaper. The address was far from exquisite.

"Just off the Mile End Road," he explained.

He watched her go with a little smile that was both gloating and worried.

Rocking-horse Antique Exporters occupied Unit 5 of St Mark's Way. Most of St Mark's Way seemed to be unredeemed bomb-site. Lady Portia parked her Metro City on large broken bricks. Unit 5 was a warehouse with huge rusty steel warehouse-doors, with a smaller door set into them, swinging open in the brisk east wind.

Inside, it was even colder. Rows of seatless worm-eaten once-elegant chairs hung on hooks overhead, like carcasses in an abattoir. Rows of wardrobes and dressing-tables stood on parade down the long dark aisles, tilting their broken mirrors like unwanted guardsmen. Two men were loading dusty Viennese wall-clocks into a container, piling them up as if they were small, ornately carved coffins. Lady Portia had never seen so much beauty so distressed.

The men ignored her till she spoke to them sharply.

"Guv'nor's at the far end."

The guv'nor ignored her, too, till she spoke. He was busy hammering a drawer back into a Georgian chest with massive blows of the flat of his grimy hand; a filthy cordless telephone lying on top jumped into the air with every blow. He was not a type of dealer she'd met before, in spite of her long connoisseurship. He had the hunched stance, wrinkled forehead and hollow cheeks of an unsuccessful ex-boxer. He weighed up Lady Portia's pale grey fur hat, sheepskin coat with matching fur collar and exquisite pale grey tights, as if he was doubtful of making a bid for her. Then he said: "Watch where you're walking. Don't sue me if you get those mucky."

"The mirror," said Lady Portia, in a voice that might have cut an armoured knight in half.

He shrugged, and led her to the darkest corner.

It was the real thing. Lady Portia knew it in her bones, even before she took in the pitted dusty grey surface that only gave back half the light it received, the swirling swags of vine-leaves and grapes, and the putti with hieratic golden-eyed gestures and missing feet. For twenty years she had been searching for the real thing, and she knew it when she saw it.

"How much?"

"We're getting five thou for it. Dollars."

"Shipping Invoice?" Lady Portia put out her hand sharply.

The man shrugged and pulled the invoice from the pocket of his dusty-brown warehouse-coat.

"It says three thousand here!"

The man just shrugged again. He didn't seem to care about his reputation. He didn't seem to care about anything.

"I'll give you three thousand. Pounds."

The man shrugged again, as if nothing mattered one way or the other.

"Provided," said Lady Portia, "you deliver today. Here's my address."

Shrug.

"And it's so *cheap*," said Lady Portia, irritated. "Why didn't you send it to Christie's or Sotheby's? Is it stolen? No, don't tell me; I don't want to know." For suddenly the idea of not having the mirror was unbearable. In that grim abattoir of beauty it shone out like . . .

"A good deed in a naughty world," said Lady Portia out loud.

The man just shrugged again. "Mind your clothes on the way out," he shouted after her.

So it was all the more infuriating when Lady Portia discovered, on reaching her Metro, that there was a long smudge of black soot on her pale-grey sleeve.

But she still drove home like a young girl for whom life was just beginning.

The mirror was up. In her bedroom; specially hung by her specially summoned joiners, who came instantly and cost the earth. And no sooner was it up than it began, as is the way of all things of true artistic virtue, to criticize every other object in the room.

She had hung it above her long low Regency writing desk, which was a fine piece in itself. The desk had survived the mirror's assault, but only just. The mirror made it look real, but thin and mean. In the end, she knew the desk would have to go. Two fine repro Hepplewhite shieldback chairs, made for Harrods in Edwardian times, had already been banished to the box-room as unbearable. Only the Georgian clothes-press held its own, in a rustic faithful sort of way, like an elderly beloved Labrador going to fat.

Lady Portia sat at her desk, looking in the mirror. Could her own beauty stand up to it? Which was a very odd question to ask. She had been thought a beauty once; but twenty-five years of marriage to Lord Copfield had long since driven such thoughts out of her head. Why should such thoughts return now, when she was well past forty?

And yet, if anything, the mirror seemed to flatter her. In its blurred dim pitted surface, the wrinkles round her mouth did not show. Only the good bone-structure, the long neck, the huge eyes seemed ... enhanced. It was almost as though the mirror knew she was its mistress and was fawning on her.

The room behind seemed darker, longer, lower – but of course everything, in the reflection, was in its rightful place. It was just the poor reflective qualities of the old worn polished steel.

There was a cursory tap, and the door in the mirror opened and Lord Copfield came in. He was home early for once; she was annoyed to be found sitting at the mirror, like a vain dreaming girl....

She noted with some satisfaction that the mirror was not equally kind to her husband. No mirror could have been. Six foot four, with huge feet and hands to match, flaming red crinkly hair, and huge horn-rimmed spectacles perched on a long pale probing nose. He looked well enough on a platform behind a battery of microphones, addressing the CBI; but in a bedroom he was as outlandish as a dinosaur. What those secretaries and systems-analysts saw in him. . . .

He sat on the bed, wrinkling the counterpane; which always annoyed her. He did it most evenings; it had annoyed her for twenty years.

He looked up and noticed the mirror.

"More ancient rubbish?" He had always hated antiques; his office was a sea of stainless steel and curved plastic. He came across to pick detailed faults. He even got as far as saying "It's *broken* – this cherub's foot. How much did you pay?" when he caught sight of his own face in the mirror.

He stared at himself; he took off his massive horn-rims. He began slowly to turn his head from one side to the other, as if . . . admiring his long-nosed profile. Those large pores in his nose . . . it was absurd, sickening.

She said sharply: "Would you mind going and getting changed? I want to get dressed."

With an effort, he tore himself away; put back his horn-rims; seemed to shake himself out of something.

"All right, dear," he said vaguely, and turned towards the door, half-falling over a chair at the foot of the bed.

He had always been clumsy; his clumsiness was not of the endearing variety.

*

Over the next week, the mirror continued to draw her. She turned the writing desk into her dressing table, and had the old dressing table – an early Victorian piece that had once seemed to possess some virtue – taken away. She found herself taking longer and longer at her *toilette,* spending hours brushing her long fair hair (which was only greying a little in front) and studying the mystery of her face, of her eyes, in the glass.

Feelings stirred that had not stirred for twenty years. She began to see herself as a lover would see her – a lover in the mirror. The brush of her clothing against her body excited her. She dreamt that the door in the darkness of the mirror would open – then laughed herself out of it – then fell to dreaming again. At least she had kept her body in shape. She could still get into the dress she had married in. A little bonier, perhaps, but. . . .

But every time the door in the mirror did open it was always the true reflection of Lord Copfield, coming home early again. He came home early three times in the next week; stood behind her, as she sat at the mirror, and stared in fascination at his own reflection. When she could bear his proximity no longer, and got up with an indignant wriggle of her bare shoulders, he would take her place, and remove his horn-rimmed spectacles and turn his head this way and that, preening. She began to feel she could not call her room her own.

Then he cancelled a weekend engagement; and came to her room ridiculously early on the Saturday morning, clad equally ridiculously in a rich old brocade dressing-gown, and some dark leather slippers with a gold pattern stamped into them. The slippers might have been attractive on some young man, but in size twelve they looked like gilded gondolas, and suspended on the end of Lord Copfield's long white bony shins. . . .

And then, after twenty years, he made a pass at her. She was so totally taken aback that it almost succeeded. She might have philosophically lain back and thought of England, as she used to do . . . except Lord Copfield kept pausing to stare at the mirror. And not even lasciviously, as she had heard was done in the brothels of Amsterdam. No, almost pleadingly, as if he was trying to prove himself a great lover. To something or someone in the mirror. . . .

She remembered Mr Lipfriend's odd remark about the mirror "keeping Lord Copfield home for a bit". She would dearly have liked to question Mr Lipfriend further. But that would have laid her open to his ridicule, and that of his loathsome friends. Instead, she took to sleeping in one of the guest-bedrooms. Though any time Lord Copfield still deigned to go to his office found her back in her old room at the mirror, mooning and brushing her long hair. She was letting it grow longer; she wanted a new style. But somehow nothing her hairdresser suggested could please her. She did not know what she wanted. A memory, the ungraspable memory of a hairstyle haunted her.

And then one day, after a particularly unsatisfying time at New Hair Inc., she remembered. No wonder she'd had such difficulty remembering the hairstyle. It wasn't on a living woman; it was on a bronze statue.

It gave her a watertight excuse to go round and see Mr Lipfriend.

He seemed more pleased than usual to see her; almost effusive. She realized she'd let her weekly visit to his shop lapse since she bought the mirror.

But she was much too shrewd to mention the mirror. Let him bring the topic up. She concentrated on the statue.

"How much did you say it would be?"

"Two thousand," he said hopefully.

"I wouldn't dream of more than seventeen hundred," said Lady Portia. "It's only the hairstyle that intrigues me. I'm thinking of getting my hairdresser to try it out on me. Having the statue to show him would be much simpler than trying to explain."

Did Mr Lipfriend give a sudden start? Had he, in the discreet spotlighting of his shop, turned perceptibly paler? Was that sweat on his upper lip? Did his hands tremble as he packed the statue carefully and took her cheque?

But she still said nothing. She was turning to go, the figure under her arm, when Mr Lipfriend asked suddenly: "How's the mirror?" It seemed to her he asked with real anxiety.

"Oh, it looks very well," she said. "In my bedroom. It's a nice old thing. I'm getting quite attached to it."

After she said the word "bedroom" there was certainly sweat on Mr Lipfriend's upper lip. He said – she thought rather desperately – "If you ever feel like selling it, Lady Portia, I could make you a very good offer . . . that would show you a real profit. . . ."

"Are *you* offering *me* a profit, Mr Lipfriend? Are you feeling unwell? You do look so *pale*. . . . " She let hope bloom in his eyes, then dashed it.

66

"I wouldn't dream of parting with it. It's quite a member of the household now."

She sensed he had wished her harm and was now regretting it.

"I could make you a clean thousand on that mirror." He was practically pleading, the sweat a sheen over his whole plump face.

"No. But if I ever do decide to part you shall have first refusal. It's keeping Lord Copfield home very nicely, as you said it would."

She thought he was going to faint. Fully satisfied with her revenge, she turned and left him.

As she was passing out into the High Street, he mumbled something after her.

"What was that, Mr Lipfriend?" she called back gaily, the statue under her arm.

"I just said," he stammered, "that that statue came in the same job-lot as the mirror."

The man sounded quite desperate. It was only long afterwards that she realized how much he was trying to warn her.

She returned from New Hair Inc. two days later, and ran up to the bedroom with the statue still under her arm. She put it on the writing desk, and compared its hair to hers. New Hair Inc. had managed pretty well, though they'd had to use lots of spray and conditioner to give her hair enough body. Her young man said no living woman could have such a wealth of hair; it was a trick of the sculptor, not drawn from real life.

She looked at the statue's bronze plumpness, then at her own clothed self. She was too thin; she was sure she was too thin. On an impulse she undressed swiftly.

Grabbed up a towel and, after a couple of ungraceful staggers that brought home to her that she was over forty, achieved the pose – and looked coyly in the mirror, as if seeking its approval.

She did not get it. The mirror showed her she *was* far too thin, scrawny. By comparison with the statue's apple-like breasts, hers sagged emptily. Where the statue had a fold of becoming plumpness across the belly, she simply had a crease, arid and unpromising as a dried-up river-bed. The mirror made her look at herself, item by item. The stringy muscles of her creased neck; the shocking deep caverns of her salt-cellars; the leanness of her thighs.

She wept. She wept because she knew the mirror was rejecting her. The mirror did not desire her; she would never dare expose herself to it again.

Then, being a fairly sensible woman, she dressed quickly and got on with other things. And abandoned the mirror, and the whole bedroom, for ever.

Its effect on Lord Copfield was quite the opposite. His hours at the office grew shorter daily. He was always home by three, and no longer went away for weekends. Once home, he vanished into the bedroom with the mirror, locking the door behind him, only emerging for increasingly scrambled meals. Often in that awful brocaded dressing gown and those ridiculous slippers. Too shame-making, in front of the servants.

Often, he brought a book to the table and read. Large, dark, nasty-looking books he would never talk about or let her see. Once, he brought a pile home and left them on the hall table while he took an urgent telephone-call. She idly picked up the top one, and opened it. It seemed to be in Latin, but in heavy block-printed German Gothic lettering; with some rather weird engraved illustrations involving beasts with strange heads and geometrical figures....

The next moment he had returned, and snatched it rudely from her hand. And gone upstairs to the bedroom, without a word. About that time, he took to locking the bedroom door, whether he was in there or not.

The number of telephone-calls escalated. Most were from Lord Copfield's office, needing urgent decisions on important problems. The worried business-voices, usually male, said things like "He *promised* me a decision before he went home tonight".

She didn't enjoy those calls at all. They required an increasing amount of banging on that bedroom door; and then Lord Copfield would come out in a blazing temper, and deal with the enquiry in about thirty seconds flat. She began to wonder if his business would survive; trembled for her supply of money to buy antiques.

But the other kind of call she enjoyed. The female calls that also pretended to be calls from his office but sounded not frantic, but miffed. Such luscious female voices, typical of the world of business, trying to mask their increasing frustration. Lady Portia greatly relished answering them with saccharine incomprehension, while their frustration declined into growing despondency and then fell silent. She never disturbed Lord Copfield's mysterious researches for *that* sort of call. She even felt a little gratitude towards Mr Lipfriend. He had kept his word, for once; the mirror was doing all he had promised.

And then, late one evening, came an urgent call from New York. She hammered and hammered on the bedroom door, and got no reply. Really, such a fuss; it was lucky it was the servants' night out. She finally choked off New York by saying Lord Copfield was out; when she *knew* he was in.

Then she went back, quite coolly, to the locked bedroom door and the silence behind it. She was rather pleased at remembering the old trick of sliding a newspaper under the door, pushing the key out of the inside of the lock with a hairpin, and drawing out paper and key together.

She went in, called out, stared around. The room had changed a lot. Lord Copfield's discarded clothes lay everywhere, jumbled up with the horrible dark books, and even some bottles and cups, full of odd-coloured liquids.

But the main difference was that he had pulled her Regency writing table away from the mirror. So the mirror looked oddly like an ornamental gilded window you could step through. And on the polished parquet floor in front of it lay the ridiculous size-twelve slippers, looking as big as barges in their emptiness. And the ridiculous dressing gown lay dropped on top of them as if Lord Copfield had just stepped out of it. . . .

And stepped naked into the mirror.

For nowhere in the locked room was there any sign of him; he wasn't a man you could easily hide.

Lady Portia raised her magnificent eyes and looked into the mirror. And, just for an instant, the room reflected was not her own bedroom. But a room panelled to the ceiling in dark wood, with a huge half-tester bed with rich dark-red hangings. There was a hump on the bed. And as the hump heaved rhythmically she caught sight of the back of a head; with red crinkled hair.

It seemed that Lord Copfield had achieved his heart's desire.

The next moment, the room in the reflection was her own room again, perfectly normal apart from reflecting the wild confusion of clothes, books and bottles. She reached out and touched the mirror; it was cold and hard and pitted steel, immovable.

She spent the night in a maelstrom of excitement. Ten times she picked up the phone, then put it down again. It wasn't that there was no one to tell; there was *nothing* to tell. A pair of slippers lying by a mirror is not evidence of anything but domestic untidiness. If she told friends, she would simply lose friends. If she told the police, there would be tappings of heads behind her back at best, and the funny farm at worst.

And, besides, she was not distressed but excited; a pendulum of excitement that swung from one side to the other. On the one hand, if Lord Copfield did reemerge, she was in possession of a magic event that she had seen with her own eyes and proved with her own hands; she alone had unlocked and locked that door. A kind of secular and unholy miracle; her own occult Shroud of Turin.

If, on the other hand, Lord Copfield chose not to return, she was ... free. Free of his large gawky frame crumpling up her bedspread when he returned from another of his amorous trips; free of his secretaries

71

giggling in the background; free to spend his considerable fortune on whatever antiques she liked. She might even go into business as a dealer herself. There'd been several who'd been willing to take her into partnership; but Lord Copfield would never have approved of his wife *working*.

She checked the room every half hour. Then, towards dawn, every hour. She could not sleep, though she had enough wit to change into a nightdress, slippers and négligé, and rest on her bed, in her new bedroom, in between times.

By ten the next morning, the phone was keeping her occupied; it rang with increasing frequency as the hours passed and Lord Copfield's business empire felt increasingly the lack of his master-hand. But all she had to say was that he was not in the house, and she had no idea where he was, which was all perfectly true. Lady Portia disliked telling unnecessary lies. And of course her statements were believed. People knew Lord Copfield's erratic personal life only too well.

She knew it was only a matter of time before someone suggested contacting the police. But they would be slow to suggest it; tactful, very tactful. Meanwhile, the compassion in the telephone voices deepened subtly. People were thinking that old Copfield had really gone off the rails this time; truly done a bunk.

Anyway, she was quite unafraid of the police coming with their questions. She had only to tell the truth. That she had last seen him fully dressed in the hall at half-past six the previous night. What kind of evidence was a smudge of crinkly red hair, seen in the distant depths of a pitted steel mirror?

After all, there were no incriminating clues for them to find. No body, no bloodstains.

On the second day, she did tidy up the room; hung the ridiculous dressing gown in the wardrobe; placed the ridiculous slippers by the bed. Piled the dark books into gaps in the library shelves, and the bottles and cups in the handyman's cupboard.

For the latter act, she did think to wear gloves.

By the third day, she no longer expected him back. She began to get bored with visiting a bedroom where nothing ever looked any different. If he returned, he would soon let her know, no doubt. She took the afternoon off to go shopping.

When she got home in the dusk, she dumped her parcels in the hall. The servants' radio was booming up the narrow stairs from the kitchen. Suddenly uneasy at her long absence, she went straight up to the bedroom.

She swung the door open; she had given up locking it by then.

There was a new smell in the dim darkened room. A smell of sweat, stale sweat. Male sweat. And the faint whiff of . . . a butcher's shop.

In the gloom, something glimmered palely, like a great overthrown statue lying on its back. . . .

She closed the door swiftly and locked it behind her; lest one of the servants come past. She put on the light.

In the cruel glare of the overhead fitting, she saw that without doubt Lord Copfield had returned. He was lying sprawled at the foot of the mirror, as if willing hands had dumped him there. And, equally certainly,

73

from his long pale waxy nose pointing at the ceiling-light to the yellow soles of his bare feet, Lord Copfield was stone-cold dead. He looked bigger dead than he had alive. He seemed to fill the floor, leaving no space to walk. And from his mountainous bony chest protruded the handle of a dagger. It had entered directly into the heart, under the apex of the fifth rib. It looked the work of someone who knew exactly what he was doing; there was only the slightest spot of blood on the yellow flesh. He had died instantly.

In a crueller, less swinging world than ours, Lord Copfield had paid the price of his sins. Lady Portia, ever the connoisseur, had just time to note the pattern on the handle of the dagger. A gold handle, with cross-pieces, beautifully and intricately engraved by a master-goldsmith, and set with clusters of red stones that glinted like rubies. Perhaps, she thought with a crazy giggle, it might have come from the hand of the divine Benvenuto himself. . . .

Then she fainted.

She came to, lying across Lord Copfield's huge disgusting sweaty feet. She got up and sat on the bed hugging herself, trying to gather her wits and fend off the waves of terror that threatened to engulf her.

It was not that she had loved him; or even felt the weary tolerant fondness of ten years ago. He had simply become a nuisance in death, as he had become a nuisance in life.

But much worse than a nuisance. She was innocent of his death; but that wasn't going to help her. Here he lay in her old bedroom; in a room the servants knew she'd kept locked for several days. She'd been the last person to see him alive. The servants, butler and housekeeper, man and wife, were practically inseparable, and would give each other an excellent alibi. As, indeed, they *should*. ...

They had no motive for killing him, of course; he hadn't even left them anything in his will. She had several excellent motives: his money, his endless philandering. She could just hear the judge's summing-up, see the newspaper headlines. Even if they thought it a crime of passion, she'd get at least five years. And she had once smelt the smell of Holloway Prison. She would kill herself rather than endure the smell of Holloway Prison.

Downstairs, the second gong sounded for dinner.

It steadied her as nothing else would've done. She went to her own room quickly, taking the key with her; changed for dinner in a couple of minutes and made up her face in one, using extra rouge to hide her paleness; and went down looking no more remote than she often did.

And amidst the supporting formality of dinner she began to think. Only one thought made sense, but one thought was enough.

Mr Lipfriend had got her into this.

Mr Lipfriend must get her out of it.

She retired to the drawing room for coffee, and poured herself a stiff brandy. And took up the cordless phone. She got Mr Lipfriend on the third attempt; just when she was again hovering on the verge of screaming.

"Your Ladyship?"

There was a shoulder-hunching wariness in Mr Lipfriend's voice that steadied her wonderfully. Mr Lipfriend had been *expecting* trouble from her.

She sailed straight in with her best and only punch.

"Mr Lipfriend – the mirror!"

He gasped, faintly but audibly. Then silence, as she waited patiently.

"Is something wrong with the mirror, Lady Portia?" Try as he might, he could not disguise the shaking in his voice. She kept silent. "You know I've offered to buy it back from you. Five thousand ... maybe I can go to five thousand five. ..."

"You seem very keen to have it back, Mr Lipfriend."

"Well, I've got this very good customer. ..."

Liar, she thought.

"It's too late for *that*, Mr Lipfriend," she said with ominous coldness. "Something rather dreadful has happened in connection with that mirror. ..."

He cracked. He said in his broadest cockney: "Oh Gawd, not *again*!"

She returned to her silence.

"What's it done?"

"A dead body, Mr Lipfriend."

"What ... who?"

"Lord Copfield himself."

That was too rough; it panicked him. He went into a blurred garble about the mirror being sold in good faith and without warranty or provenance.

"Mr Lipfriend ... if, thanks to your mirror, I get ... sent down for murder ... I shall certainly drag you down with me. I shall tell the truth, even if I'm laughed

76

at. I shall hire a private detective to trace the recent history of your mirror. I wonder which other ... ladies and gentlemen have ... disappeared ...?"

She'd certainly hit the nail on the head there. He said, "Oh Gawd," again, even more desperately. Then he said: "I'll be with you right away, Lady Portia." Then he added: "Well, give me a couple of hours to make arrangements."

That was his undoing. She had an unpleasant vision of Mr Lipfriend making for the Channel ports, with his passport in one pocket and the enormous wad of notes from his safe in the other. Never to be heard of again.

But at the same time she saw the way through.

"Lord Copfield was killed by a dagger, Mr Lipfriend. It is still embedded in his chest. It appears to be made of gold, and set with clusters of rubies. To my inexperienced eye, the workmanship appears to be Florentine, of the sixteenth century. *Very* fine. Perhaps the work of the divine Benvenuto, Mr Lipfriend. There appears to be a family crest engraved on it. A rampant bull. Wasn't that the crest of the Borgias?"

The dealer struggled with the coward in Mr Lipfriend. And won. A mounting excitement crept into his voice.

"It sounds like.... Is the handle about six inches long, bound with gold wire – very thin?"

"Yes, Mr Lipfriend." She had no idea; she closed her eyes delicately as she lied.

"One went like that at Sotheby Parke Bennett ... Paul Getty Museum ... grossed five hundred thou...."

"If you remove the body, Mr Lipfriend, the dagger will leave with it. I have no use for daggers."

"I'll have to clear the whole room, Lady Portia – a job-lot, carpets an' all. First thing in the morning suit you?"

"That will suit me very well. On condition you come here tonight and make me an offer. In *front* of the servants – and, Mr Lipfriend . . .?"

"Yes?"

"I want a half-share in the sale of the dagger. Only I can give it provenance. It's been in our family donkey's years, of course. Nobody thought it at all valuable – Grandy used to open his letters with it. You spotted it when you came to buy the other stuff. . . ."

"I'll give you forty per cent," he said nastily. That was when she knew she was home and dry.

"Done," she said. She would miss the Georgian press; but perhaps she could buy it back at auction through a discreet agent.

In the world of antiques, you can get anything moved at a price. The men who came to clear the bedroom brought a huge plywood case, to pack the framed watercolours by the elder Crome, in their ornate gilt frames.

It seemed rather heavy for gilt, as they staggered back downstairs with it. But the butler and his wife were being questioned by Lady Portia at the time about an apparently missing silver pot-pourri bowl. They were so relieved when that turned up in a drawing-room cupboard that they never noticed the packing case being carried down a second time. . . .

A week later, on the company secretary's advice, she reluctantly called in the police. By then the bedroom had been entirely refurnished by Harrods.

Through the long police inquiry into Lord Copfield's disappearance, Lady Portia often wondered where his large and inconvenient body lay. Certainly he would never lie in the family vault at Highgate. But, about that time, the last flyover of the M25 extension was finished, with massive piers of poured concrete. A flyover that would bring the entire motorway to a halt for a month, if any attempt was made to demolish it. . . .

That thought was the source of great security to her, as she got on with directing the new and flourishing export business of Copfield & Lipfriend.

The Borgia dagger was a sensation at Sotheby Parke Bennett in New York. The Getty made a new record by paying five hundred and fifty thousand dollars for it, even more than they'd paid for the first. But, then, the Getty is always creating new records. There was a little difficulty getting an export licence; but authorities at the V & A said that in the end it could not be considered a national treasure, being foreign in origin.

The Girl Who Couldn't
Say No

As she grew older, Joanna didn't think much of the
gifts her fairy godmother had bestowed. Did she *have*
to shoot up to five foot ten? She barely kept her place in
the hockey team, by agreeing to go in goal and be shot
at. Of course the netball mistress loved her, saying she
could just reach up and drop the goals in. There had
even been a facetious offer from the boys' basketball
mob. . . .

And did her neck have to grow so long, and her
profile so snooty? And her eyes so large and dark? That
greasy weirdo Furnival, in the Arts Sixth, had had the
cheek to tell her that her eyes looked *tragic*. And had
written her a poem that she had read once, torn
up and burnt.

Nevertheless, that didn't stop every boy in the Sixth
referring to her as "the Duchess". Even the younger
staff, who specialized in being matey, had tried calling
her "Duchess".

She wanted to scream at them all that she hadn't
changed inside; that she was still as happy, friendly,
come-day-go-day as she'd always been. But they
wouldn't take any notice. They preferred to believe the

evidence of their eyes; that way they could make more funny cracks.

She stood naked before the mirror, as she so often did these days, wishing she could shrink. She'd tried to make herself look smaller by stooping her shoulders – till the PE teacher had a friendly word about permanent stoops not being attractive, about being *proud* of the way she was made. She'd stood proud since; it made her look taller still.

She inspected herself, item by item, and couldn't really find any fault. Except her figure would never look with-it at a disco. She looked more like a classical statue in the grounds of some stately home. All she lacked was a pedestal. She might as well be a statue, distantly admired, out in the cold with bits of moss and lichen growing all over her. At least if she was white stone instead of pink flesh it wouldn't *hurt*.

Oh, to be thirteen again, and the same size as everybody else; with her hair plain red instead of, as Furnival had written, divinely auburn. Thirteen again, and just good at lessons, without a thought for the future. Instead of in the Upper Sixth, without a clue what she wanted to be.

Everybody else knew, of course. Daddy wanted her to be an accountant in his firm. Mummy wanted her to be a famous investigative journalist. The careers teacher was talking about becoming an actuary, and the mathematics of higher risk.

She wanted to please everybody; but you *couldn't*. Somebody was going to be disappointed and cross, whatever she did. . . .

She looked out through the double-glazing. It was snowing again. She suddenly shivered and went goose-pimply and started to get dressed. Just as Mummy yelled up the stairs: "What are you *doing*, Joanna? I want you to go to the library...."

Oh God, not the library *again*.

Mummy stopped typing, and pushed her spectacles up on to her hair, in that way that was so with-it five years ago. Mummy produced a magazine for the local unemployed, meant to teach them their rights and be a thorn in the side of the Thatcher government. Actually, Joanna thought it more likely to make the unemployed rude and offensive, and make life a misery for the over-worked Social Security people. But she never said so.

Sometimes Mummy thought she was Soft Left, and sometimes she thought she was Old Labour; her hero was Sir Harold Wilson, with whom she had once been photographed on the High Peak Walk, which celeb-rated annually the victory of socialist ramblers over Tory landlords and gamekeepers in the 1920s. The photograph was on Mummy's desk. Both Mummy and Sir Harold wore open-necked shirts under sports coats, very long shorts and long socks. They both carried knobbly sticks. Mummy looked young and radiant; Sir Harold merely pensive, sucking his pipe.

Now Mummy pointed to the tower of books on the right-hand side of her desk. Green papers on Housing; white papers on Unemployment; Government Acts of 1954. Mummy was a thorn in the flesh of the public library, too.

"Better take my rucksack," said Mummy. The sacred High Peak rucksack, of course.

"Can't I use the grip?"

"The grip will make your shoulders droop to one side permanently."

"I change hands. . . ."

"No, you don't. You always end up carrying it in your right . . . and you'd better wear my boots . . . the snow was very treacherous when I took Harold for his walk."

Harold, the Labrador, sitting roasting his backside at the electric fire, gave a gracious flick of his tail. He even looked like the real Sir Harold: a little concerned for the future of the nation, but bearing up bravely.

"I shall look a real fright," objected Joanna.

"It doesn't matter what you *look* like . . . and wear my bobble-hat – that snow *clings*."

It wasn't worth arguing. By the time she had it all on, and her own anorak, she looked as if she was about to climb Everest.

"Oh, and there's some cleaning to take to Tarrant's – there'll be room in the rucksack."

With a sigh, Joanna went. The snow was falling heavily and lying treacherously, and she was glad of the boots and bobble-hat. She just hoped she didn't meet anybody. Otherwise there'd be cracks about Chris Bonington and Sherpa Tensing, and did Mallory and Irvine really make it to the top. . . .

She had joined the main road on the outskirts of Lancaster when the funny thing happened. A lot of traffic was passing her, northbound into Cumbria. The rucksack was heavy, and she put her right hand to ease the strap. Her hand sort of slipped as she brought it away, and she *might* have jerked her right thumb in the air. . . .

There was a slithering screech of brakes, and a large and expensive black car slid to a standstill in front of her. The driver leant across, a mere blur through the snow, and wound down his electric window and looked out.

Joanna liked his face instantly. A lot. The laugh-wrinkles, the bright blue eyes, the neat silver hair. She always liked or disliked people on sight, and had never found herself wrong.

"Hop in, young lady. How far you going?"

She *said*, "Just to the library", but she was fumbling, with her head down, getting out of the rucksack-straps; she thought afterwards he mustn't have heard her straight. Anyway, she was glad of the lift; the library was nearly two miles away, and the snow *very* treacherous.

The car started off smoothly. The man shot her a nice grin, and she gave him one back. Then he said: "I do admire today's young people. Here am I, feeling all sorry for myself, hating the snow; and here's you, heading for the high hills and high adventure . . . "

She thought he was making a joke about her rucksack, so she just gave him another nice grin.

"I used to be a great climber," he added wistfully. "Thirty years ago. You wouldn't think to look at me now I've climbed Great End under ice in a blizzard. We had to cut steps with ice-axes, every inch of the way." He sighed. "Haven't had my boots on for fifteen years – too busy making damned money. And what *for*, I ask myself."

And he was off into the past, happy as a lark. The cottage at Seathwaite, where you got the best tea in Cumberland. Thirty years ago. That nasty little ridge between Scafell and Scafell Pike, where he'd seen fifty members of the Manchester University Classics Society hit by a snow-squall without warning. "Ran all over the place, screaming. Silly young girls. Not a spare

85

sweater or compass or torch or pair of boots among them. Not like you, m'dear. I can see you're the real thing, know what you're doing. No flies on you. . . ."

It began to dawn on Joanna that he really thought she was a real climber. But just then they came to a T-junction. Left for the town centre, cleaner's and public library. Right for the M6.

Before Joanna could open her mouth, she was heading north up the M6 for Cumbria.

It was weird. She couldn't do a thing, except let herself be carried north. He was so happy, you see. So lit up, living in the past. She couldn't bear to ruin his happiness and lose his admiration by telling him she was just going to the public library. The look of let-down and contempt on his face would have been too awful; he would have brought her back in disgrace, a fool and a fraud. Too awful. Anyway, she could always hitch-hike back, once he'd dropped her.

But he wasn't disposed to drop her easily. Not only did he talk mountaineering non-stop – snap-links and piton-hammers and crampons. But he also turned off the M6 at Kendal, to show her the pub where they always met in the old days. In his delight at finding it almost unchanged, he took her in for a late coffee. Had she tried Switzerland yet? The Matterhorn was only a tourist-trap these days, with old ladies and their dogs being hauled up by guides by main strength, but Mont Blanc still had some unspoilt places. . . .

Then it was lunch at Grasmere. She was afraid he would ask her questions about mountaineering that would expose her as a fraud; but he was far too busy telling her the best escape-route off Great Gable.

As they climbed back into the car, it was well after

three; more snow was falling, and it was starting to grow dark. And his dream of mountaineering was starting at last to run out of steam.

"Run you as far as St John's in the Vale," he said. "Then I must off for the M6 and Glasgow. Big day tomorrow, selling toilet-rolls by the million. What a life, eh? Rather be going up a mountain with you. Which one you doing first? Skiddaw?"

"Er . . . Yes."

"Try going up from the north, m'dear. South side's bloody boring. Just a muddy pudding. . . . You'll be all right if I drop you off here, then? Soon get a lift into Keswick. And Keswick Youth Hostel was always half-empty this time of year . . . thirty years ago . . . so you'll be all right for tonight. Righty-oh. Nice meeting you. Nice to be with a real climber again. Haven't enjoyed a day so much in ages." He got out and opened the car door for her, helped her settle her rucksack on her shoulders, did a neat three-point turn in a farm gateway and was gone, a brief blur of headlights in the thickening snow and gathering gloom.

She was struck by the sheer ridiculousness of life. She was suddenly paralysed, dropped from his warm genial dreams into a cold hard world, with a rucksack full of Green Papers and Mummy's cleaning and, as she soon discovered when she came across a phone-box and thought of ringing Mummy, not a penny in her pockets. Oh, well, she could reverse charges. . . .

But when she got into it she found that even in rural Cumbria phone-boxes get vandalized.

She trudged on towards Keswick; because that was what he had expected her to do. His coffee and lunch slowly turned to a cold tight hard ball of anxiety in her stomach. She saw farmhouses, with telephone-wires leading to them. But how could she ask to use the phone? She had no money to pay, and they would look at her strangely.

After that, even the farmhouses ran out. It got darker; the snow got deeper under foot, and the rising wind drove it cruelly into her face. She knew she ought to be worried about prowlers; but she was so cold she was past worrying. A wilderness of cold and dark and trudging; feeling more and more unreal.

She felt like weeping, but she couldn't. She just trudged on. Mummy must be worried sick about her; she'd been gone five whole hours. Mummy would be phoning Daddy at the office; phoning the police by this time.... Oh, it was all so *awful*....

She heard a car coming up behind her; the first car for ages. She half-turned, with a blind imploring gesture. She knew you shouldn't go in cars with men, especially after dark....

The car braked sharply, swerved on the snow, nearly hit her. A little Morris Minor shooting-brake, headlights glaring through the falling flakes. It looked a harmless sort of car. But that was silly. How could you tell by the look of a car what kind of person was driving it? Probably rapists drove all sorts of cars....

Again, a window was wound down, and a voice said sharply: "Well, do you want a lift, or don't you?" A voice so deep and gruff it might have been a man's.

But, thank God, it was a woman's.

"Books?" said the woman as she took the rucksack. "Where on earth are you going, out here at this time of night, with all these books?"

"The public library."

"*Which* public library?"

"Lancaster public library. . . " And then it all came tumbling out.

"Gracious me," said the woman. "I've heard of gels doing stupider things; but not many. You're nearly frozen stiff. You'll catch your death if we go on sitting here. You're coming home with me. A stiff brandy is what you want. Then a cup of tea. And we must ring up your mother. . . ." She had a nice voice – brisk and bossy, and yet tolerant of all the foolishness of gels and men and dogs and horses. Joanna just sat back and let it all start happening again.

Eventually she found herself sitting on a chintzy sofa in a rather large, gracious room, sipping her brandy and fending off the attentions of two large and over-familiar black Labradors. And listening to the woman talking to Mummy. She could even hear Mummy's incredulous and indignant yelps. But the lady in thick tweeds and stout brogues was being more than a match for Mummy.

"Of course she can't come home tonight. She's nearly frozen stiff. What she needs is a good hot bath."

Squawk, squawk, squawk from Mummy. The tweedy lady merely swept her aside.

"Believe me, I know Cumbrian roads and Cumbrian weather. Your husband would be a suicidal fool to start out tonight. You have my word I'll put her on a train safe and sound tomorrow morning. . . ."

Squawk, squawk.

"Of course you don't know who I am. My name is Helen Harris. *Mrs* Helen Harris. If you have any doubts of my intentions, ring the Keswick police. I happen to be a JP on the local bench. Yes, Helen Harris, and my number is Keswick 28965. Now, if you'll excuse me, I think I'd be better employed seeing to your daughter. Who is *quite* safe, I assure you. Yes, Keswick 28965. Write it down. Yes, I will wait while you find a pencil – *I* always keep one by the phone."

Joanna kept on wondering whether she should go and talk to Mummy. But the quality of Mummy's squawks boded ill. She would have to try to explain, and Mummy wouldn't give her a proper chance, and she'd just make a fool of herself again. Much easier to sit by the fire, letting the heat soak steamily into her jeans, and playing with the dogs' ears. Mrs Harris seemed quite capable of dealing with Mummy.

Joanna let her eyes wander round the room; it was not the sort of room she was used to. The carpet was very pretty and unusual, but worn bare here and there, and the worn parts covered by even prettier rugs. Beneath their chintz, the chairs and sofa sagged down into comfortable shapes, like friendly old horses. But there were beams across the ceiling; real oak beams, not like the plastic ones the Hankinsons put in, to cover up the girders where they'd run two rooms into one. And dark panelling all the way up the walls, instead of Vymura. And pictures of people everywhere. Black-and-white photographs in polished silver frames of people who by their dress must have been dead for some time; and dark huge oil-paintings on the walls, of people who must have been dead a great deal longer. And a grandfather clock with a very slow tick and a brass pendulum that passed and repassed a little oval glass window in the case. She felt she was sinking down into the sofa; sinking down into a much slower, older time.

She must have dozed, because Mrs Harris was suddenly shaking her gently, saying: "Bath! We must get you out of these wet clothes!"

She followed her upstairs like a lamb. On the landing, another grandfather clock was pouring out that older, slower time all over the house. A house full of the smells of polish and flowers and old leather and a brass bowl of pot-pourri on an old oak chest dated 1623.

The bathroom was incredible. The bath, run and steaming, was a huge cast-iron thing that stood on feet like a lion's. The handbasin was cased in polished mahogany and so was the loo, with a little porcelain handle to pull, right next to the seat.

"I've put you here – in the bedroom next door – my daughter's old room. I've put out some of her pyjamas and her old dressing gown. They'll do at a pinch. Dump your wet stuff outside the door, and I'll hang it over the Aga."

Before Joanna could stammer "Thank you", Mrs Harris was briskly away downstairs.

Joanna peeled her revoltingly damp clothes slowly off her steamy skin and put on the dressing gown. It was old, like everything else in the house, but snug. Green tartan; a dressing gown that could have been used by any member of the family without disgrace. She mooned round the room; stared into the fire set and lit in the old iron grate, bright but as yet giving no warmth as the pale yellow flames leapt through sticks and paper. Stared at the narrow bed, the shelves with moth-eaten teddy-bears and rabbits and copies of *Mr Jeremy Fisher* and *The Wind in the Willows*. She felt she was slowly becoming the other girl. There was a black-and-white photograph on the bedside table. Must have been taken when she was about eighteen – the kind of photo you saw in county magazines at the dentist's. She looked a bit like Mrs Harris, but prettier, with her hair in a page-boy bob. About 1965, perhaps. . . .

Suddenly she thought the girl might be dead. With a shudder she fled to the bathroom, and tried to soak such thoughts away. Why should she be dead? Why shouldn't she just be married and living away? Or married and living in the same village?

A sharp rap on the door summoned her from such thoughts.

"There's a cup of tea in the sitting room when you're ready!" Mrs Harris's voice was friendly, but full of a new authority; Mrs Harris had *really* taken charge.

Her wet clothes were gone from the landing floor. Joanna suddenly felt lost, as if her soul had gone with them. She went downstairs and huddled warily in a corner of the sofa.

The tea-service was silver; old silver, hand-chased and dented. Not at all like the Hankinsons' catalogue-silver, let alone Mummy's no-nonsense stainless steel.

"They fit you, then?" Mrs Harris observed the dressing gown and pyjamas with satisfaction. "You're nearly as tall as Fiona was; a well-made gel. Can't stand what these modern gels do to themselves – starving till they're walking skeletons. Princess Diana could set a better example."

"Is . . . Fiona . . . living away from home?" asked Joanna timidly.

"Heavens, yes . . . away . . . married . . . three children . . . she'll be forty next year. They're out in Southern Rhodesia – can never bring myself to call it Zimbabwe, though I suppose I should. Husband farms. These are my grand-children." Photographs passed, reassuringly in full colour, driving away the ghosts. Joanna didn't mind standing in for a *living* girl. So they were snug with chatter about the wildlife of Southern Rhodesia, and the inconvenience of boarding a Jumbo at Salisbury airport, until Mrs Harris suddenly said: "Do you dance, my dear?"

"You mean . . . ballroom dancing?"

"I certainly don't mean that other stuff."

"We had ballroom-dancing lessons in the Lower Sixth. I can manage a bit."

"I don't suppose – no, it would be unfair to ask you. . . ."

"What?"

"I don't suppose you'd like to go to a hunt ball tonight? No, you must be tired. I wouldn't have mentioned it . . . only my son . . . is being difficult about going. He doesn't live round here, and doesn't know any of the gels, and hasn't anyone to take. Only . . . we've always gone . . . we always took a big party when Barney – my husband – was alive. We haven't missed a year since 1947 – the year of the big snow, and we couldn't get the old Morris started." Her tough big-nosed face was suddenly wistful; and beneath the deep lines Joanna could see the young wife of 1947.

"Yes . . . all right . . . I'll come." Her dancing wasn't very good. But she was willing to make a fool of herself for Mrs Harris, who'd been so very kind. After all, however big a fool she made of herself, she'd be gone tomorrow, safe home, and no one round here would ever see her again.

"Thank you, my dear." Mrs Harris suddenly looked twenty years younger, as her face lit up. Then a trace of doubt crossed it. "I only hope . . . my son's manners will be up to yours. He can be a bit of a trial . . . full of London ideas. I think he only comes home . . . to make fun of people. He's bright . . . he lectures . . . but I don't think it's made him a very happy person. Well, let's go and see what we can find you to wear. What size shoes do you take? Eights? I think we can manage. Fiona seemed to dip and dodge between seven and a half and eight."

And so they went up to the great dark wardrobe, with its full-length bevelled mirror. And Joanna preened and posed herself through the years between 1965 and 1970. This was how her mother might have looked, if her mother had cared for such things, instead of trogging out to Aldermaston, all anoraks and boots and CND banners. Image after image swam up at her, out of the dark depths of the mirror, with the shadowy attentive figure of Mrs Harris lurking behind. Each image different, for each hunt ball. But in each of them Joanna looked mysterious, pale, with big dark eyes. Every inch the Duchess, she told herself wryly. And yet she felt she had come to her place; a place where women were mysterious and beautiful, and men stood by to open doors for them or take their wraps from their bare shoulders. It made Mummy seem such an angry scrubby bitter creature. . . .

"Of course they're all frightfully old-hat," said Mrs Harris doubtfully. "But it's all quality – and young people seem to like old-fashioned clothes these days. Don't they buy fur coats from Oxfam?"

"They're all beautiful," Joanna whispered. "But I like the white one best."

"You have champagne tastes, my dear. That was the year we could stretch to Hartnell. You'd better take it off, so I can check it for stains and press it. But first. . . ."

Her hands came from behind, round Joanna's throat, and there was a triple row of what, from their shimmer, must be real pearls.

That was, for Joanna, the biggest moment. But, typically, the biggest moment broke. There was a voice, an uneven angry voice, calling up the stairs.

"Mother? Isn't *anybody* home?"

"Come down and show him," said Mrs Harris with spirit. But there was a distinct tremor in her voice.

She came downstairs with a care that made her stately, lifting the hem of the white gown so it wouldn't trip her. There was a plump man standing at the bottom of the stairs, his hands pushed down so hard into the pockets of his old car-coat it seemed he wanted to rip the pockets out. His hair was black and too greasy, so it hung down in strands around his face; the face of a scowling cherub.

He looked up at her, and, just for a second, the scowl faded into a look of distinct admiration. Then – and it was quite horrible – he smashed the admiration from his face as deliberately as a child might scrawl on a wall or an adult rip up a letter, and put the scowl back.

"Who the hell are you?"

"Joanna Dalby," she faltered, and came to a standstill three stairs up. She caught the smell of his breath; he'd been drinking, but he wasn't drunk. She heard Mrs Harris say, behind her: "Miss Joanna Dalby, who has kindly agreed to be your partner at the hunt ball tonight, Roger. Though it's more than you deserve." It was said bravely, but that tremble was there again.

"I'm not going to any hunt ball, partner or no

partner. The unspeakable in pursuit of the uneatable..."

"Don't be tedious, Roger. That wasn't even funny when Oscar Wilde first said it. They are my friends, and they were your father's friends."

"So what? That doesn't mean *I* have to mix with them."

"Only a couple of hours, Roger. For old time's sake...." Mrs Harris was close to tears.

"*Fuck* old time's sake."

Fury came to Joanna's rescue. She glared down at Roger from the superior height of five feet ten and three stairs. "I'll come with you, Mrs Harris, even if *he* won't."

It seemed to shake him. "All right. I'll put on my bloody penguin-suit *for old time's sake.* And spend the time in the bar. At least we all share a táste for Johnny Walker." He pushed past Joanna rudely and went upstairs.

"I'm afraid he doesn't look well in evening-dress," said Mrs Harris with an attempt at lightness. "He doesn't so much look like a head waiter as like a student working in his vacation." But she was still close to tears. She came down and hugged Joanna with great warmth. "Thank you, my dear."

They went in Roger's car. An E-reg Saab, but so strewn with books and papers you could hardly sit down. Roger wrenched at the wheel, stamped on the accelerator and brake as if the Saab was a wild animal and he was trying to strangle it with his bare hands. Next to him, Mrs Harris in a mink of rather elderly cut sat in silent disapproval. Not a cosy journey; Joanna feared that at any moment the police might appear and breathalyse him.

Still, from the back seat, there was magic. The snow had stopped, the moon was out, turning the white fields and crowding hills, the dense fir plantations and grey skeletons of oaks into a temporary fairyland.

Withens Hall lay sheltered on the south side of a steep hill. The park was full of sheep, and Joanna could swear she saw a few deer lurking under the oaks. The sheep were huddled round great square bales of brown fodder that had been broken open for them like crumbling Oxo-cubes.

The Hall was two-storeyed, long and low. Under its thin powdering of snow, the stone-slab roof sagged with the weight of centuries, between gigantic chimneys. Long rows of little windows, and every one seemed lit. The sound of music drifted over the snow as they parked on the far edge of a mass of Land Rovers and their Japanese competitors. It was funny, walking through the carpark, wearing wellies and holding up her dress, with her silver slippers in a Sainsbury's plastic carrier. But Mrs Harris was doing exactly the same, and so were the women in the other parties they joined up with. Lots of murmured greetings; Joanna had to shake hands with dark blurs many times. Roger was pretty rude to everybody; but they seemed used to him and found him hilarious, which didn't improve his temper.

He waited for them, while they changed their shoes in a stone-flagged room marvellously hung with dog-leashes and moth-eaten army greatcoats. He even stayed with them long enough to mumble a few words to their hosts, Lord and Lady Mulberry. (Surely, thought Joanna, they couldn't *really* be called *Mulberry*; nobody was called *Mulberry*.) Then, with a grunt, he was off for the bar.

Lady Mulberry pulled a wryly humorous face. "I suppose that's the last we shall see of *him*!" Then she smiled at Joanna. "At least you won't be too bored, Miss Dalby. We've got something new for the young set this year – a disco. I *do* so hope you enjoy yourself. And keep your eardrums intact."

She smiled with great charm, and passed them on professionally, to make way for the next party.

Mrs Harris stared at Joanna in some distress. "I didn't know about this disco business. Are you going to stick with us old fogies, or plunge into the towering inferno?"

"I'll stay with you," said Joanna desperately.

So Mrs Harris found her cronies, and sat and yattered; and Joanna sat with her, trying desperately hard to hang on to the ends of a near-incomprehensible conversation about speying bitches when they were past breeding, and a particularly intelligent fox who had recently given the Ladies' Meet a hard time in light mist, getting most of the hounds lost by finally wriggling under a tall barbed-wire fence and going away over Mr Marshall's.

Then she became aware that a middle-aged gentleman was standing over her; and even more aware that he was asking her to dance. She got up all in a flurry, and was greatly relieved to find that her feet seemed to know what to do of their own accord, so she was able to concentrate on what the gentleman was saying. He was talking about his daughter, who was away at college learning to be a farm secretary. His talk flowed smoothly; all she had to do was smile at times, and to say "Yes, I see" at others. Then the gentleman asked for the young point of view on this and that, drugs and four young things living together in a flat that was more like an uncleaned hen-coop than civilized living. Beyond his gentle kindness she sensed a very real anxiety, and did her best to say reassuring things.

After that, she had a succession of middle-aged and elderly men. Most tried very hard to please; most seemed deeply baffled at the way their offspring had turned out. She felt she was turning into a dancing Telephone Samaritan, giving advice on what to buy for birthday presents and how to see that daughters did not turn anorexic. In a weird way, she began to enjoy herself. It was only the odd remarks she kept hearing out of the corner of her ear that brought her to the edge of blushing.

"An absolute stunner...."

"Wish *I* was thirty years younger...."

"A real old-fashioned girl ... didn't know they made 'em like that any more...."

"I wish our Simon would bring home something like that."

"Such lovely manners ... came with young Harris."

"Where is the young fool, then? Wasting his time in the bar?"

She sparkled, knowing she was approved of. It brought pricks of tears to her eyes that total strangers should look after her so well.

All but one: a fat man of forty, with a red sweating face and thick lips, who danced very badly because he'd had too much to drink. He lurched; she had to hold him up or he'd have fallen. He had no sense of rhythm, and trod on her feet. Worse still, he not only asked if she would let him take her out to dinner some time, but his sweaty hand kept landing on the bare part of her back and somehow sliding down on her covered buttocks. She was aware of people starting to notice; she blushed helplessly with the shame of it. And again she was near to tears. The others had been so nice. Why did he have to spoil it? What did he think she *was*?

The third time his hand strayed on to her bottom, he pinched her, then leered at her, looking her deliberately straight in the eye.

Rage froze her rigid. She just stood absolutely still and stared at him.

Now it was his turn to look embarrassed; he mumbled: "Come on, my dear, be a sport." He tried to push her back into motion, but he was too drunk and clumsy. She locked her legs rigid, and resisted with all her young strength.

Now everybody was staring at them. She was utterly shamed, but she still would not dance one more step with him. For a long moment his dull green drunken eyes stared at her; he tried several more appeals.

Then he dropped his arms and fled across the dance-floor in a series of tipsy swerves and vanished through the door.

"By God," said somebody, "she froze old Toby out, what? Serve him bloody well right."

'She's a cool 'un, isn't she? Gave him a look like a duchess. . . ."

Then another of her grey-haired admirers came swiftly to her rescue and swept her back into the dance, talking especially gently and lightly.

Talk of her must have got around; instead of dancing with the fathers, she found herself dancing with the sons, who presumably had abandoned the towering inferno in her favour.

She did not like them half so well. Where their fathers had been confident, they were uneasy. They did not hold her securely, as they tried to whizz her round; they trod more often on her feet; they were not very good dancers at all. And they were even worse conversationalists. It was all about the money they were making or intended to make. Or about cars that were all GTIs and had twin carbs. Or they weren't going back to Tunisia next year, it was such a dump, they were going to try Thailand. . . .

On the whole, she thought dreamily, she seemed to prefer older men. Perhaps she might marry an older man. Grey hairs were preferable to spots and sweating palms. . . .

There was one nice young one who talked about his dogs. He was no older than her, and quite harmless, with newly washed fair hair that kept drifting up into tufts. He was the one who talked her into having a crack at the disco. But the music immediately drowned his pleasant voice, so she could no longer hear about the dogs and after one – well, you couldn't call it dance – she began to develop a headache and want the loo. She went through a door marked "Ladies".

That was a mistake.

It was the young crowd's loo. And the moment she went through the door she smelt trouble. The air was full of smoke, and it wasn't Player's or Silk Cut, either.

There was a huddle of girls passing a joint around and giggling, and making particularly stupid remarks. One offered the joint to her. When she shook her head violently, they all laughed with rather theatrical scorn.

And there were two girls beyond them doing something she couldn't see properly, though she thought one of them had something like a pencil up her nose. . . .

She began to back out. Then the door opened, banging into her and sending her stumbling to the far side of the room. The door-handle had taken her very painfully in the back of her pelvis. She leant against the wall feeling a bit sick and watched a most amazing sight.

There was a boy in the room. A tall thin boy, about six foot two. His long neck, with prominent Adam's apple, stuck out of his frilled evening-shirt rather like a tortoise's. But he had a nice face, very brown with a lot of freckles, and extremely blazing blue eyes. She thought it was a face that was used to being happy; but it wasn't very happy now. . . .

He advanced on the gaggle of girls.

"Give me that *thing*!" His wrist and hand were strong and brown and sinewy, and shaking with rage. "Give me that thing and get *out*!"

The girls quailed. One of them said feebly: "Oh, go on, Tree, be a sport. It's only grass. . . ."

He snatched it from her hand and ground it out on the floor.

"Oh, don't be such a wally, Tree!"

"This is my *home*. Get out!"

With much offhand shrugging, huffing and picking up of handbags, they went. The boy they called Tree stood quite still for a moment, breathing hard and rubbing his hands together as if he were washing them. He was obviously trying to get back his cool before he returned to his guests; quite oblivious of the fact that he was standing in what was, after all, the ladies' cloakroom. Joanna's heart went out to him; her glance of compassion must have tickled the back of his neck like a fly, for he whirled and saw her.

"Who the hell are *you*? Didn't I tell you to get *out*?"

"*I'm* the girl who came in to use the loo. I'm the girl whose back you practically broke, shoving a door into it...."

He was instantly all contrition. "Oh God, *sorry*. I might have known; you don't look like one of *them*." He craned round and looked at her back. "I say, you *have* got a bruise coming. Can I get you something to put on it?"

She realized how low the dress was cut behind, and blushed. "Not really. I don't want anything smelly...."

"You mean, like horse liniment?" When he grinned he was really quite dishy, in spite of his Adam's apple.

"I say, aren't you the girl who was dancing with the golden oldies?"

"Yes," she said, daring him to make a joke of it. "So what? I happen to like *real* dancing. Any fool can do the other stuff."

"All the fools are. My father was rather taken with you. Said he didn't think they made 'em like you any more."

"Bully for him." She was still touchy, but his grin was more soothing than any horse liniment.

He took her hand gently. "I think the old man got it right for once. Come and *dance*." She was appalled by the effect of his touch; felt goose-pimples run all the way up her bare arm.

They were at the door when a low giggle came from

the row of toilets. A very nasty giggle. Not a giggle that had merely been eavesdropping on them, but a giggle that was out of this world, on some Cloud Nine of its own.

The giggle came again; then incoherent mubblings.

"God!" said Tree turning pale. "That's not just a reefer. . . ."

"Two of them were sniffing something when I came in. It wasn't glue, either." Tree walked stiffly across to the loo door. "Who's in there? Who *is* it?"

Another mad giggle was the only reply.

"God!" he turned a desperate face to her. "What can I do? The Chief Constable's here, and Chief Super Hutchinson. If they find out, my father can be done for letting it be used in his house. . . ." He looked fearfully at the door, where anyone might come in at any moment. Anyone female, anyway.

But somehow she knew exactly what to do. She whipped outside and, with a lipstick from Mrs Harris's handbag, wrote "OUT OF ORDER" on the door. Then she whipped back inside with the key, and locked the door.

"God, you're a genius," said Tree. "That gives us a breathing space. Who taught you that?"

"Don't they teach you to use your loaf at public school?"

"I suppose not, really." He turned back to the still-giggling toilet. "What . . .?" He made a very English, helpless gesture with his freckled hands.

She surveyed the loos; they must ordinarily have been visitors' loos, for when the Hall was open to the public. They had open partitions, like at school.

"Give me a leg-up," she said decisively. "Like I was getting on to a horse." At the mention of "horse" his troubled eyes cleared. He made a loop with his hands for her to put her silver-slippered foot into. The next moment she was shooting up into the air like a Saturn rocket; he was nothing if not fit. She nearly went clean over the partition to land head-first on the occupant. She clung to the partition-top for dear life, and surveyed the occupant dubiously. The occupant had purple-and-silver hair, which clashed horribly with green satin dungarees. The occupant was lolling back on the toilet-seat, patting the toilet-chain and giggling at it as it swung. Otherwise she seemed fit for male eyes to rest on.

Joanna tried getting a leg over; but in the long dress it was quite hopeless.

"Can you lift my dress up?" she said, as strictly practical as possible.

"Oh, I *say*. . ." Tree sounded very shocked. Then she felt his hand lifting her dress obediently. She blushed again, at the panorama of leg and briefs she must be presenting; but glancing down she saw that he averted his face with equally blushing decency. She got a leg over, dropped inside and opened the loo door.

"Don't know her from Adam," said Tree bitterly. "Damned gate-crasher."

"Don't know her from Eve, you mean!" she said, trying to ease the tension. As his face brightened a little she felt incredibly maternal for he still looked appallingly helpless.

"Go and find one of her horrible little friends," she said, "and bring her back here. She'll know who she is and where she lives. When you come back give three pairs of knocks, so I know it's you."

"God, that's bright," he said. "You'd have made a good spy!"

She took him to the door, opened it a crack to make sure the coast was clear, and pushed him out. He went away up the dim corridor, with his long heronlike stride. She locked the door and sighed. He wasn't really dim; just helpless off the beaten track, like other public schoolboys she'd met. Once they got away from the done thing... but he was awfully sweet with it.

She went back to the giggling object, who was still patting the toilet-chain, lost in wonder. She noticed with a pang of pity that it had spots and sticky-out teeth; it could never have been very pretty, even in its right mind.

Six taps on the door; he could certainly move when needed. He slid in, a ragged piece of paper in his hand.

"They were all shooting off... they wouldn't come back to help." He sounded very shocked, as if someone had not only stolen the Crown Jewels but burped in front of the Queen while doing so. "I've got her name and address, though."

"Right – got a car?"

"Mine won't take three. But I nicked the spare keys of the old man's Roller."

"Well done, James Bond. Now, if we can force this window open...."

"I'll go and get Withinshaw to help – the butler – good sort – he won't split." He forced open the window with a controlled violence that made her shiver inside. "Stand fast – he'll be round in two ticks." He went off again, looking much better now he was in control of the situation.

In two minutes, six more knocks.

"Good evening, madam. I believe there is a snag...."
He said it so calmly it might have been a spilled glass

of wine. He picked up the snag as if she was a feather, saying in infinitely soothing tones that were a mixture of nanny and old-fashioned village policeman who has seen everything once: "Now, now, miss...." Next second, car headlights swept across the window and Tree was back. The snag was slid out and Tree stood in the glow of the headlights, holding her in his arms in an infinitely romantic way that made Joanna green with envy. Then the snag ruined the picture by reaching up and grabbing a handful of his hair and giggling....

Tree turned back towards the window.

"Hey, Joanna, you *coming*?" There was a need in his voice that made her heart leap.

Tree drove with large sure hands, dimly lit by the light of the dashboard. Joanna sat in the back with the snag, whose name turned out to be Marilyn Lumley.

"Tree?" It seemed so natural to call him that now.

"Yep?"

"Tree, she's worse. She's got her eyes shut and she's not answering and she's breathing oddly. You can't just dump her at home; she needs medical attention...."

He slammed the Rolls to a screeching halt; his head and neck were stiff as a poker; his big hands clenched on the steering wheel, the knuckles standing out in the light of the dashboard.

"God ... hospital ... it'll get out then all right. It'll crucify my father – he's Lord-Lieutenant of the county...." His voice grated and broke with sheer misery.

She said gently: "It'll crucify him more if she dies."

He took a deep despairing breath. "OK. If you say so...." She felt she held his life in the palm of her hand. Then another bright thought came.

"Unless you've got an old family doctor you can trust?"

He laughed with pure joy. "Doc Sanders. Good old Doc Sanders. He'll get us off the hook...." The Rolls shot forward, with un-Rolls-like haste; more like a young pup of a sports car.

"Leave it to me, young Tree," said Doc Sanders. "Tell your father not to worry. I'll deal with the parents. *Verb. sap.,* eh?" He glanced at Joanna. "Get your young woman back to the dance. Make the most of it while you're young, eh?"

Tree opened the door of the Rolls and handed Joanna in like a lady.

"Comfy? Like a rug?"

"Thanks, but no. I'm not a dowager-duchess yet!"

"You could be one day – or something like it."

"What on earth do you mean by that?" She gave one of her disbelieving unladylike snorts, then wished she hadn't.

He said nothing. He drove smoothly now. It was true that the loudest noise was the ticking of the clock. They went along in silence; but a comfortable silence. Then he said: "You really saved my life tonight. All our lives. You've got a lot of style, haven't you?"

She said: "I've got a certain amount of common sense." She wished she hadn't said it so sharply, but his tone of adoration embarrassed her.

He was silent again; but she could feel something growing between them, like a thundercloud. She tried to ignore it, and enjoy the majesty of the silent white hills. They passed again through the park gates; they had funny animals on top like dragons with two legs, holding shields, and a ridiculous heap of snow on top like an ice-cream cone.

"Will you have all this, one day?" She said it teasingly, trying to break up the thundercloud that was growing.

"Yes. If we can keep on paying for it. Bloody roof needs seeing to again. Bloody roof just *eats* money. You'd think the slabs were solid gold. . . ."

He pulled up the car, just short of the house, in a part she hadn't seen. All around them topiary shapes of clipped yew and great stone urns had a dressing of snow, like Christmas puddings. A keen little wind played a tune round the car windows, but otherwise it was terribly quiet. She just *knew* he was going to say something terrible and irrevocable. So when he only said, "It all depends upon the land – whether we can make the land pay enough," she could have laughed out loud with relief. But she stifled it, because he was so terribly serious and grown-up-sounding.

"We've got so much marginal land – high pasture. Keeping the bracken back's a terrible problem. But I think we can do it. I've been to college – the Royal at Cirencester. I think the old man's starting to listen to me. . . ."

What was so terrifying about that statement that it should make her catch her breath?

After a long pause he said: "It will need every ounce of savvy we can muster."

Then he turned to look at her. "All the girls I know are *stupid*. All they want to do is go off to London and help their friends run crummy little boutiques. They've got no *standards;* they smoke pot and sleep around.

Nobody wants to stay up here and make a *job* of things."

She said stoutly: "They can't *all* be like that, Tree. You're exaggerating."

So why was her voice trembling?

"I'll *never* find anyone like you again." Then, after a pause that seemed to go on for ever, he said, "Joanna, will you marry me?" – and immediately swung back and stared at the steering wheel gloomily, his shoulders hunched as if he expected a blow.

She started to talk. She told him she wasn't eighteen yet. She told him she was worried about her 'A' Levels. She told him her father was a chartered accountant, that her mother ran a free newspaper exhorting the unemployed to bloody revolution. She told him she wanted to go on to university. She told him how awful Mummy was. She talked on and on and on, but the one thing she found she couldn't say was "No". At last she stopped, exhausted. In the silence that followed, all she could find to say was: "Why do they call you 'Tree'?"

He laughed, because she hadn't been able to say no, and said: "My name – Mulberry – of course. And because I'm so tall and thin." Then he added: "Aren't you going to chop me down to size?"

The tension broke, and they both laughed. He put a large warm dry hand over hers; it was gentle and yet it was the hand of a conqueror. And she couldn't pull her hand away. All she could say was: "This is bloody ridiculous. I don't even *know* you."

"My father proposed to my mother first time they met. Mulberrys have a family tradition of love at first sight." Then he looked at the extra-thin watch on his strong wrist. "God, it's time for supper. Will you let me take you in?"

"Weren't you taking somebody else?" She felt she was being whirled along by a great river – a great river of proposing Mulberrys that went back hundreds of years. But she still couldn't say no, bear to hurt him.

"Only my cousin Felicity, and she won't mind. She's gone on a chap in the Royal Marines, but he couldn't make it tonight. I can have one of you on each arm. How's that for style? Old Fliss won't mind at all; she's a good sort – you'll like her."

The rest of the evening passed in a whirl. Nothing was said about what had gone on in the topiary garden; but everyone seemed to think they *knew* something. A whirl of the friendly smiling faces of strangers, and congratulatory handshakes; though what they were congratulating her for she could never make out. She hoped it was for saving their bacon by getting rid of the snag. They certainly all knew about that; even the Chief Constable, who now he didn't have to take notice of it officially was happy to take notice of it unofficially. Even the thin and grim Chief Superintendent Hutchinson cracked his face in a smile.

The golden oldies approved of something; even Lord and Lady Mulberry seemed to approve of something. Only some of the girls gave her *very* nasty looks, as she danced away the rest of the evening with Tree. And her mind still desperately tried to invent a painless way of saying no.

And failed. He drove her home in the Rolls; kissed her on Mrs Harris's doorstep – not with passion, but certainly with confidence. His lips were firm and dry and warm; it was a bit like eating bread fresh from the oven.

"I'll drive you home in the morning," he said, "and have a word with your papa."

Then he was gone; and she still hadn't been able to say no.

The following morning passed like a dream. Mrs Harris hugged her, before she got into Tree's ancient and dangerous-looking Ferrari.

"It's just like a fairy-tale, dear, just like a fairy-tale. I'm so *happy* for the pair of you ... of course, I've known young Tree all my life ... but I think he's a *very* lucky young man."

Even Roger got out of bed to say goodbye to her, unshaven and smelling vilely of booze.

Then they didn't go straight down the motorway. Tree took her back to Withens Hall, to drink coffee and say goodbye to his parents, in Lady Mulberry's cosy little sitting room.

Lord Mulberry had been somewhat strangulated. Apart from several times telling her she'd put up "a damned good show last night", his only contribution had been to blurt out: "You do want children, eh?"

On the point of collapsing into total confusion, Joanna had found refuge in a surprisingly cool "Yes – after I've been to university."

"Some of these modern gels – don't seem to want 'em at all." Covered with almost equal confusion, Lord Mulberry had departed abruptly to see to some guns or dogs or something. Lady Mulberry had laid a comforting hand on Joanna's arm.

"You're very young, my dear. Don't let these men rush you." But she had smiled so warmly that for once Joanna hadn't minded being told she was very young.

Afterwards, she and Tree dawdled the car through the park, making a diversion to see the home farm. Tree had talked about everything with a slight disparagement, as if he were offering her a birthday present in slightly torn wrapping paper. In a breathtaking way that made everything seem *hers*, and so enchanted under its blanket of snow.

Even the first part of the drive had been enchanted. Until she saw in the distance, sunk in the hollow of the land, the towers and chimneys of Lancaster.

And then it was awful. Suddenly quite awful. As the world she knew grew more real, Tree grew less. He babbled on happily about spending weekends, and holidays skiing and ... it all seemed like something out of a crummy Mills & Boon novelette. Her replies became monosyllabic: she could no longer bear to look at him. But, even worse, he didn't seem to notice and went babbling on in his happiness. She became terrified he might stop the car and claim a kiss. Even though he was turning into an amiable ghost, a figment of her imagination, she still didn't want to *hurt* him. And she felt a terrible cloud of pain gathering, for both of them, till she almost wished he would crash into the back of a juggernaut and end the misery.

The dreadful signs carrying the name of her home town appeared, filthy and graffiti'd among melting snow; and passed. Thank God the streets were empty, because of course, she remembered with a start, it was Sunday morning.

They passed her comprehensive; new and raw and already falling apart. What had that got to do with the ancient snow-coated slabs of Withens Hall?

Drummond Avenue. Ribblehead Drive. She just

kept on saying "Right here, left here" dully, as the end of the dream ran out like grey old movie-film.

Then they were in her road. She looked with hatred at the ugly Edwardian red-brick detached houses, the neat privet-hedges, the house-agents' signs.

In the distance, Daddy was out in the drive, in the freezing weather, cleaning his new Ford Granada. Every Sunday he did it, rain or shine, even when the washing-water threatened to freeze on the windscreen. And the light was on in Mummy's study and Mummy's red head was bent over her typewriter. Still rallying the dole-queues to revolution. . . .

"Stop," she shouted at Tree. Well, more of a hysterical scream. He slapped on the brakes so hard the car went into a nasty little skid and ended up with one wheel on the grass verge. Daddy looked up frowningly at the unseemly Sunday sound, his face a distant white blur. Then turned back to washing round the front winkers of the Granada.

And so she hung, silent, on the brink of home. Quite unable to say a word, and knowing that if Tree touched her she would scream again, and this time in earnest. She'd just *explode*, and never stop exploding until there wasn't a fragment of her left bigger than a pinhead.

But Tree sat beside her, quite still and silent. As the silence lengthened and lengthened, she grew amazed at his patience. But her mind would do nothing but play out the same two scenes over and over. Trying to introduce Tree to Daddy. Trying to introduce Tree to Mummy. Mummy, Daddy, this is Tree – the Hon. Frederick Mulberry, son and heir to Lord Mulberry of Withens Hall in the county of Cumbria. . . .

She knew exactly how they would react. Daddy would be far *too* impressed, and flap around frantically

114

after sherry and glasses, talking far too loud and as real as a three-pound note, and making the wrong kind of jokes. Mummy would go tight and white, and then start asking nasty questions about fox-hunting and what right had one man to own enough land to provide homes for five thousand working people? And then she would say that property was theft. Ten thousand pounds, Joanna would have bet, that Mummy would say that property was theft. . . .

And that would be before Tree had summoned up the courage to ask for her hand in marriage; which he certainly would in his brave old-fashioned way.

"They'll go mad," she said to herself, and was horrified to find she'd spoken out loud.

"They always do," said Tree gently. "When my maternal grandfather proposed to a Tiller girl, Great-Grandmama tried to shoot herself."

"Oh," said Joanna, impressed out of her own panic for a second. "What happened?"

"Her hand was shaking so much she missed, and smashed a priceless piece of Rockingham. Her husband sent her off to take a cure at St-Malo, and she won twenty thou on the gaming tables and came home quite reconciled."

Joanna began to giggle. She couldn't stop. Then Tree was giggling, too. Then they were roaring with helpless laughter; so that old Mr Tomlinson, passing on his regular Sunday-morning walk, peered down under the hood to see what all the fuss was about. He smiled gently at them, waved to Joanna, and passed on to let his old spaniel pee against the next tree. And somehow the dog peeing broke the spell.

There would be trouble; there would be hell to pay. But it would pass, like Tree's great-grandmother coming home from St-Malo. The question was not what they all wanted, but what *she* wanted. . . .

She looked at Tree straight and hard. His honest blue eyes, his suntan, his freckles, his Adam's apple, his large square hands. If he had been a Sixth Former, sitting next to Furnival in assembly, would she have wanted him *then*?

The answer was probably yes. Given time.

"Tree?"

"Yes?" His suntan paled. He looked positively *old*, like a man about to be sentenced to death.

"Tree, I don't want to get engaged – yet. But I do want to go on seeing you."

"Could be worse," he said with a wry grin that conquered another quarter of her heart.

"Right," she said. "Let's get it over with. Drive on, McDuff!"

Rosalie

It happened on Jane's third morning at Darlow Primary, just before break. Miss Hood, her new teacher, called out calmly, without looking up: "Who'll go to the stock room for me?"

All the class raised their heads; then sat in frozen silence. Not a hand went up. The silence went on and on.

"Oh, come," said Miss Hood, looking up, "I won't *have* this stupidity! Now, who will go?"

Jane put her hand up. It wasn't that she wanted to be teacher's pet, though she liked to be liked; it was just that the lesson was maths, the classroom walls a dull dingy brown and the old windows too high up to look out of. A trip to the stock room seemed a welcome break.

"Thank you, Jane!" said Miss Hood a bit too warmly, and her voice was full of relief.

All the class turned and stared at Jane in horror. She felt suddenly terribly alone. A group of girls round the table in the corner began muttering and giggling in that nasty sort of way.

"You can stop that nonsense, Janice," said Miss Hood sharply. The group in the corner shut up, but they went on nudging each other.

"Do you know where the stock room is, Jane?" asked Miss Hood with, again, a little too much warmth and kindness.

"No, Miss Hood."

"All the way along this corridor, turn right at the end, and up the stairs. Knock on the staff room door, but if there's nobody there go straight through and you'll find the door to the stock room at the far end. Now, off you go, before the bell goes."

Everything seemed so strange that Jane was at the classroom door before she remembered to ask: "Please, Miss Hood, what am I to fetch?"

"Oh, dear me," said Miss Hood with a little laugh. "I'd forget my head if it was loose. The big map of the world. It's hanging on the wall. Roll it up, so it doesn't trip you on the stairs."

"Yes, Miss Hood." Why was everybody staring so? It made her feel *very* odd.

Then one boy leapt to his feet and shot his hand up.

"Please, miss, I'll go with Jane. Show her . . . help her carry it. It's dead big, that map. . . ." He looked rather pale, all of a sudden, and rather sweaty, like boys do before they fight. He was called Derek something. And Jane knew he was sweet on her already, from the way he'd been staring across the room at her. But he looked quite nice; not one of those who try to drag you into the boys' toilets. . . .

"I'm sure Jane can manage without your help,

118

Derek," said Miss Hood sharply. "If you're so keen to go, you can go by yourself."

"Please, miss – *no* miss!" Derek sat down like a deflated balloon, paler than ever. He gave Jane a despairing look, as if she was going to prison or something.

"Off you go, Jane," said Miss Hood firmly. Her head in a whirl, Jane went. Down the long, long corridor, with classrooms on her right, where younger kids huddled round tables or listened to their teacher wearily, already thinking about the Kit-Kat they were going to buy at break.

Round the corner and she was in a windowless brick passage, so dark that an unshaded light bulb burnt there all day, and the kids' coats hung in rows like their bodies. The friendly burble from the classrooms was cut off, as if by a knife, and Jane felt lonely without it.

Grey concrete stairs led up to the staff room, and a grim Victorian iron hand-rail with iron knobs set on top of it, as big as marbles, to stop the Victorian boys sliding down it at break. She climbed; the clatter of her shoes was the only sound in the silence.

It said 'Staff Room' on the door, in paint so cracked and yellow it might have come from Tutankhamun's tomb. She knocked. No answer.

She knocked again to make sure. It would be terrible to walk in and have a teacher pounce on her without warning.

Still no answer.

She went in. There was nobody there, but it felt as if somebody should be. A two-bar electric fire struggled, feebly cherry-red, against the December cold. There was a kettle on the gas-stove in the corner, on a low light but singing to itself and puffing out a little jet of steam. Some teacher must have nipped up and put it on for the coffee at break.

And spread around the room were little piles of teacher. Here, a bunch of exercise-books lying open, with a red Biro on top. Here, a shopping-basket full of old Sunday supplements, with a pair of furry boots alongside. Seven heaps because there were seven teachers, besides Mrs Winterbottom, the Head, who had her own study. It made Jane feel a bit spooky, like Goldilocks when she got into the house of the three bears. She wanted to have a nosy, but she didn't dare.

And there was the door at the back, marked 'Stock Room' in the same cracked yellowing paint. Jane opened the door, and got a fright because it was as black as pitch in there. Shaking, she groped for a light-switch and finally found it.

But she wasn't in the stock room yet. She was in a corridor without a ceiling. Overhead, she could see the rafters all grey with cobwebs, and the roof with long strips of cement holding on the slates and trying to keep the wind out. Trying, because the December wind was whistling through; making queer noises like a boy whistling between his teeth. And on each side, in the shadows where the roof sloped down to the floor, were piled dusty old netballs, shrunken with age and lack of wind; and tennis-rackets with black broken strings; and old hockey-sticks done up with bands of adhesive tape.

And at the end of the corridor *another* door marked 'Stock Room'. She had a sudden fear that if she opened that door there would be another room, with another door at the far end marked 'Stock Room', and so on and so on. . . .

She was halfway up the corridor when she distinctly heard a voice say in her ear: "And that's the way rain is made. . . ."

She whirled in terror. But there was no one there. The voice came again.

"Books away," it said. It sounded, in a ghostly way, like a teacher's voice. Jane ran back to the staff room, giggling with relief (and rather afraid a teacher's hand might suddenly reach round the door and turn the light off and close the door and leave her in the pitchy dark).

But when she got back into the staff room there was no one there, only the kettle singing softly to itself. She even opened the far door and looked down the concrete stairs, but there was no one in sight.

But the piles of teacher lying about cheered her up and told her not to be silly. So back she went, and this time she got as far as the stock room. And pushed open another door on to pitchy dark, and reached round and switched on another light and. . . .

A hideous face leered down at her. A whole row of hideous crumpled and cracked faces. . . . She gave a little squeak before she realized they were papier mâché and powder paint; pirates and goblins from some old school play. The whole stock room was full of old school plays. A golden crown hung over a golden chair with only three and a half legs. There was a dusty backdrop painted with trees that looked like furry lollipops, full of bright black-and-red birds like a currant-cake.

And there, thank goodness, was the map of the

world. She was just able to reach up on tiptoe and unhook it. As she did so, another voice spoke in her ear.

"The old saying is quite true. An apple a day *does* keep the doctor away...."

And then there were other voices, children's voices, singing some song she could not recognize. Because it was half-hidden by the wind whistling through the slates next door, like a boy whistling between his teeth.

She stared around in terror – at the jumble of shadows in the windowless room, at the old wicker baskets with piles of purple curtains dropping out of them. And beyond, at the end, *another* door. A door with no name on it opened a crack into blackness.

Then the voice in her ear said: "Where's Jane got to?" And she was running in a blind panic, out of the stock room, along the dark corridor, through the empty staff room where the kettle sang, and down the concrete stairs, with the unrolled map of the world slowly wrapping itself round her legs like enfolding arms.

She felt herself falling. She screamed. Then it all went black.

Jane was bored. At first she'd been glad the cottage hospital had given her a room of her own, away from the nosy old ladies. But after eight hours she'd have been glad of the nosiest old lady. All she had was a headache, two scraped knees, and a long and curiously straight bruise across the front of her ribs that was turning blacker every time she looked at it. But she had to stay in bed because of possible concussion. The room was horribly hot and dry, the jug of water on her bedside locker lukewarm; tea had been yuk hard-boiled potatoes and yuk mince, worse than school dinners, and the hospital's idea of reading-matter was copies of *Woman's Own* from 1984.

Everyone told her cheerily she'd be as right as rain tomorrow, so why wasn't she allowed up? Mum had only called for ten minutes, on her way to book-keeping evening-class, because Mum was determined to become a chartered accountant even if it killed her. Jane turned again to the problem page of *Woman's Own*. But it was all letters from mums who were tired of dads.

A yakky Cheshire voice echoed down the corridor.

"We've come to see the little girl," said the voice loudly and apologetically. Jane, at eleven, sincerely hoped it was not she who was being referred to.

"Our Derek made me come. He insisted. I think he's a bit sweet on the young lady in question. He even washed his face and combed his hair without being told. Eeh, love's young dream. . . ."

"Shut *up*, Mum," came Derek's desperate voice. Then they were in the room. Derek did look unusually clean and combed; his hair was as wet as a seal's.

"Hello, dear," said Derek's mum. "We've come to cheer you up! My, you do look a real picture, lying there. No wonder our Derek's so—"

"*Shut up, Mum!*" Derek's face turned scarlet, below his seal-like pelt.

Still, Jane was glad her own mum had fetched her best blue nightie with the lace on the collar. And that her hair lay long and combed and heavy across the lace.

"How you feeling, love?" asked Derek's mum. "They

say that concussion's a terrible thing . . . people can die of it . . . and your first week at your new school, too. . . . What a shame when you were just getting settled in. . . . Derek's brought you grapes *and* flowers . . . spent all his pocket-money at the Offie—"

"Look, Mum, go an' wait in the car, will you?"

"*Gratitude!* I don't know why I bothered. Only he was frightened they wouldn't let him in without me—"

"*See you later, Mum!*"

"Oh, all right. I'll go and cheer up poor old Miss Herbison, seeing I'm not welcome here . . . the poor old soul's on her last legs, they say . . . still, at eighty-seven she's had a fair innings. . . ."

Derek heaved a sigh of relief at her departing steps. Then he gave Jane a look of gleaming-eyed excitement that had little to do with romance.

"Did you *see* her?"

"Who, your mum?"

"No, stupid, the ghost in the stock room!"

"What ghost?" said Jane scornfully. But her heart suddenly hammered, at the memory of the voices, and of the wind in the slates, like a boy trying to whistle between his teeth.

"The ghost of Rosalie Scott. She haunts the stock room. At school. We were sure she'd got you, when you didn't come back. There was a boy sent up there once, on a errand, who *never* came back. Rosalie got him. He's still up there somewhere. In the roof."

"Don't be so *silly*," said Jane, very rudely, because her heart was hammering painfully against the long bruise on her chest. "There was no ghost. I just tripped over the map I was carrying, and fell downstairs. I forgot to roll it up, like Miss Hood told me."

"Oh," said Derek. He seemed deeply disappointed that the ghost hadn't got her; Jane began to wonder whose side he was on. There was a long silence on both sides till Derek said: "Want some grapes?" He let her snap off a small bunch; but kept the bag on his knee and began to dip into them himself, with some gusto.

Jane felt a certain waning in his interest. So she asked: "What about Rosalie Scott, then?"

"She was a kid in the top class. Ours. Yonks ago. She was riding her bike home from school. She was knocked down. By a steamroller. Flattened as flat as a pancake when they picked her up. And she'd been dead scared of going on to Shackfield Comprehensive after the summer holidays. So when she was dead she went straight back to our school an' she's been up in that stock room ever since."

"That's *stupid*," burst out Jane. "If she was dead an' could go anywhere, why didn't she just go home?"

"Her mother didn't want her – she had too many other kids."

"And this boy you said Rosalie *got*? What was his name? Where did *he* live?"

"Dunno," Derek chewed on some more grapes morosely, and then didn't know what to do with the wet pips, so first looked at them, floating in the palm of his hand in a pool of spit, then shoved them in his pocket and wiped his hand on his jeans.

"There, y' see?" said Jane, rather wondering what she meant herself.

"Look," said Derek. "This was yonks ago. People have forgotten his name, it was such yonks ago. But he's still up there, with Rosalie."

"But the teachers ... the police...."

"The teachers *know*, but try to kid us they don't exist. Why d'you think Miss Hood sent *you* up? None of us would go...."

Jane remembered the funny way Miss Hood had sounded. "Oh, that's *horrible!*"

"Yes, it is," said Derek, mumbling over some more pips. "It's all right if you go up there in twos. You still hear her, but she can't *get* you. That's why I volunteered to go up with you. But the teachers won't let us go up in twos – they just say we're being silly. But they *know*...."

He finished the grapes, shoved the bag in his pocket, gave her the bunch of flowers, saying, "Here y'are," with another blush. Then he added: "I'd better go. It's 'Brookside' night – me mum can't bear to miss it."

And with a squeak of trainers he was gone.

The following morning, the doctor felt Jane's forehead, took her pulse, jabbed a thermometer painfully under her tongue and announced she was as right as rain and could go home.

Jane gave him a *very* funny look. She'd hardly had a wink of sleep, because every time she closed her eyes she was back in the stock room with the bobbing horrible masks; and Rosalie Scott, as thin sideways as a penny, as a photograph, would come swimming out of the door that led only into blackness....

On finally being woken up, she had looked at her face in the mirror as she washed; she had the most terrible blue shadows under her eyes that might have been fascinating and romantic at any other time....

Breakfast had been yuk porridge, with watery milk. The only good news was that Uncle Geoffrey was coming to fetch her, because Mum was at work.

Uncle Geoffrey was her fabulous beast. He was terribly tall – six foot three – and as thin as a teenager, and walked along with great bounding steps like a heron in a hurry. From the side-view, he was very like a heron, with his great thin beaky nose and mass of crinkly wavy grey-black hair that he combed back with loads of Brylcreem to Aunt Bridget's despair, especially in the matter of pillow-cases. He made a lot of money writing ghost-stories of a nice English kind, full of stingy undertakers and phantom coffins that floated about on their own and punished the baddies till they reformed their evil ways. He lived in a great rambling house with two staircases and endless cellars that was very good for playing hide-and-seek in on Christmas Day. And he always knew just how much to frighten you; he could make you scream one minute, but you were laughing the next because you knew it was him all the time.

Mum called Uncle Geoffrey her Rock of Gibraltar; they had moved up north to live near him, when Mum and Dad got their divorce.

Jane heard his great booming voice, the moment he came through the hospital entrance. Then, amazingly, she heard Sister actually laughing. It seemed a kind of special magic, to make Sister laugh. Because, although Sister was no older than Mum, she had sharp lines round her mouth and was *extremely* strict. But when Sister walked in with Uncle Geoffrey she was not only laughing; but she looked quite lit-up and pretty. Jane supposed it must be because Uncle Geoffrey was slightly famous, and had appeared on the Box four times.

Anyway, Uncle Geoffrey asked how his favourite niece was, picked up her overnight bag with one little finger, and took her out to the car, which was ancient, but very black and shiny: a Daimler, as Jane had learnt to tell her friends. Inside, it smelt comfortingly of leather, Aunt Bridget's eau de Cologne, and Uncle Geoffrey's evil little black cigars. Jane had to move a battered pair of binoculars, two cat-collars and a copy of *The Times* from the front passenger-seat before she could sit down, but that was quite normal.

"School, then?" asked Uncle Geoffrey as he switched on the ignition and whoomed the engine far too much and far too noisily, so close to the hospital. "Might as well get back to it, eh?"

"I suppose so," said Jane in a very small voice.

"What's up?" asked Uncle Geoffrey.

Jane just let it all come out. Uncle Geoffrey was that sort of person. When she'd finished, he said: "God, how fascinating! *That's* how myths grow. I must write that all down before I forget the details."

"What you mean, *myths*?" asked Jane, feeling both relieved and grumpy that he was being so cheerful. "You mean like the Norse myths and legends?" Uncle Geoffrey had given her a book on Norse myths and legends last Christmas that had been quite interesting. "What I just told you is *true*!"

"Yes," said Uncle Geoffrey, still all lit-up. "And, you see, there *was* a girl called Rosalie Scott. And she *was* killed on her bike. Though not by a steamroller – by

128

quite a small car. So of course she wasn't at all as flat as a pancake when they picked her up. It must have happened ... let's see ... about fifteen years ago. Your cousin Robert was at the school then, though not in the same class. There was no talk of ghosts in *his* time; he'd have told me if there had been. I must ask him, when he next rings up from Saudi. ..."

Jane's world just collapsed. It had been bad enough before, when Rosalie Scott was just a *story*. But now she was *real*. She sniffed desperately; but the tears were streaming down her face like a hot trickly curtain.

"Oh, come, this will *never* do," said Uncle Geoffrey, pulling into the school yard and putting on the handbrake. "We can't have you in *this* state. I'm going to sort this out straight away. Stay in the car ... no ghosts here – only the Hound of the Baskervilles in the boot, of course, but I've given him a rubber bone. ..."

Jane watched him stride away across the playground and vanish inside. She seemed to wait a terribly long time; every kid who went past going to the outside toilets stared at her like she was some freak, and that only made her feel lonelier. Then he came back, walking with Mrs Winterbottom, and it was clear from the way that Mrs Winterbottom was smiling and laughing that his Great Charm had worked again. He opened the car door in high good humour.

"Out you get, young lady – we're going up to the stock room to sort this out." He looked at her white face. "Up we go, all three of us. I don't think the school ghost will play up your headmistress – not if it knows what's good for it."

129

Up the concrete steps Jane walked, with the ramrod back of Mrs Winterbottom in front and the creaking leathery steps of Uncle Geoffrey behind.

But even with them in front and behind she did not feel safe.

They whisked her through the empty staff room, like she'd heard that in France they briskly whisked murderers to the guillotine, saying it was the kindest way. Then they were in the ceiling-less corridor, full of shrunken dead netballs. And that boy was still trying to whistle through his teeth. . . .

"That's the wind in the slates, of course," said Uncle Geoffrey. "But you'll have worked that out for yourself, bright girl like you. . . ."

Then the first voice came, eerie as ever. But rather unfairly it said: "Put down your pencils, all of you, and pay attention."

"You know who that is, don't you, Jane?" said Mrs Winterbottom, rather as if she was putting Jane through a very severe assessment-test she must not fail.

"Yes, Mrs Winterbottom. It's Miss Hood."

"Your own form-teacher. And, what's more, in case somebody says something silly, Miss Hood is quite a *new* teacher at this school; she was not here in Rosalie Scott's time. And *that*", she added, as a new voice came, "is that wretched Amanda Higginson in 2A, being rude to her teacher again. I'll have a few words with *that* young woman. And there's 1B practising tomorrow morning's new hymn. . . ."

"It's the ventilation system, love," said Uncle Geoffrey, with a kind sad smile that seemed to have seen everything under the sun. "You know those big grilles you have in the classroom ceiling? They lead up into big metal ducts that carry the hot used air from the classroom to the roof ventilators. And, being metal, they carry the voices from the classroom as well. That's all it is. But it *is* a bit eerie."

"That, and some *very* silly girls," said Mrs Winterbottom severely. "Like that Janice Woolley in your form, Jane. Silly girls who have nothing better to do than make up ridiculous stories to frighten people with. Oh, I could *smack* Janice Woolley for the misery she's caused the other girls. And the more sensitive boys, too."

"Right, Jane, that's it, then," said Uncle Geoffrey. "We've taken you seriously, treated you like an adult, and expained. Are you satisfied?"

"Yes," said Jane. But, deep down, she wasn't.

"Off you go, then – back to work. Miss Hood's lesson sounds most interesting," said Mrs Winterbottom.

The third night, she awakened from her first nightmare screaming, before Mum had finished watching the ten o'clock ITV news. Mum wrapped her in her dressing gown and a blanket and drove her straight round to Uncle Geoff's.

Uncle Geoff's sitting room was so deeply cosy it was enough to banish even her nightmare. Three large cats blinked amiably from the backs of old leather armchairs. There was a roaring log-fire that made the shadows dance cheerfully on the reddened walls. Uncle Geoff had his carpet-slippers on, another cat on his knee, and a glass of whisky at his elbow. Aunt Bridget jumped up from knitting her intricate Fair Isle jumper to switch off the sad boomy music on the record-player. Jane suddenly felt a hysterical little fool.

But all the faces took her seriously.

"Now, Jane, tell us the lot," said Uncle Geoff.

"It's those girls – Janice Woolley's lot. They say Rosalie Scott is after me, now she's seen me. They say Rosalie's mad at me because I told you, and you told on her to the Head. They say Rosalie's going to get me. They say she can leave the stock room an' come an' get me *anywhere*. In the classroom, in the yard, in the toilets, even at *home*." Jane felt the stupid hot blinding tears starting to trickle again.

"Hey, Jane," said Uncle Geoffrey. "Let me show you how the world wags."

"What you mean?" sniffed Jane.

"Let me make a few guesses. Tell me if I'm right. This Janice – is she a big fat girl?"

"Yes!" gasped Jane, shocked out of her grief.

"With legs like tree-trunks?"

Jane giggled; she didn't have to say yes.

"And spots?" asked Uncle Geoffrey. "And none of the boys ever gets sweet on *her*?"

"The boys call her Woolly Elephant. . . ." Suddenly Jane was laughing as helplessly as she'd been crying. Uncle Geoff was a wizard.

"Well, now," went on Uncle Geoff, "how do you think Janice Woolley feels about a pretty girl like you? Who the boys *do* get sweet on?"

Jane blushed; she did like being admired – even by Uncle Geoffrey who was quite *old*. "You mean, she's *jealous*?"

"Even Janice Woolley has to get her kicks from somewhere. Oh, yes, Jane, somebody hates you; some-

132

body's out to get you. But it's not Rosalie Scott; it's Janice Woolley...."

It almost comforted Jane; it almost fitted. And yet....

"But *all* the class is saying it," she said, and the tears threatened to return.

Uncle Geoff went thoughtful, dreamy, his head resting on his hand and his eyes far away. "The power of a good story," he said quietly, almost to himself. "A good story has power, Jane. Even when there isn't a word of truth in it. I should know. But I'm going to make you up a better story – a better story than Janice Woolley's. And that should fix her...."

He was silent for a moment. Then he said: "Is there an outhouse in your school – somewhere in the yard where the caretaker keeps his tools and paint and toilet-rolls and such?"

Jane nodded, feeling suddenly excited.

"And has it got a door that's a bit rotten at the bottom – with a gap or a hole near the bottom?"

Jane nodded again. How could he *know* such things?

"And a rather old rotten wooden floor? Right. Now, let's say there was an old caretaker at your school ... in your cousin Robert's time. What shall we call him? Some fairly common name...."

"Smith!" suggested Jane.

"No, that's *too* common – like Jones and Brown and Robinson. Nobody believes stories about Smiths and Joneses. No, let's call him Mr Buckley – that's a good local name, but not *too* common. I can see him now, with his cap on his grey hair, and his pencil – a yellow pencil – behind his ear. And his brown bib-and-brace overalls, and his old sports coat, so old it had gone grey with chalk-dust. . . ."

And it seemed to Jane that now she could see Mr Buckley, too. She held her breath at such magic.

"Now, one day, Mr Buckley was in his outhouse, sawing up old netball-posts to make logs for his fire – with one of those hand-held mechanical saws – and his hand slipped, and the saw cut off his other hand at the wrist. . . ."

Jane saw it all so clearly she nearly screamed.

"Steady on, Geoff," said Aunt Bridget.

"I know what I'm doing," said Uncle Geoffrey, nearly breaking the spell. "Anyway, poor old Mr Buckley ran into school holding his stump of an arm, which was all pumping blood like a watering can. And the Headmistress put a tourniquet on his arm to stop the bleeding, and he was rushed to hospital, and his life was saved. And afterwards he went to be a . . . nightwatchman . . . in . . . Manchester . . . because with only one hand he wasn't able to be a caretaker any more. . . ."

Jane gulped with excitement. It was just the sort of ghastly story that Janice Woolley loved.

"But," said Uncle Geoffrey, "in all the excitement, everyone forgot about the *hand*. And it fell down a hole in the floorboards, and there it stayed, slowly withering and getting all green and grey and *thin*. . ."

Jane gulped again with horrible excitement.

"And," added Uncle Geoffrey with a flourish, "after a bit the hand got *bored* being down in the hole, and came back to life and crawled out of the hole slowly, like an old crab, thinner and greyer than ever. And it crawled out through the hole at the bottom of the door...."

Jane paused for breath; and looked at the faces gathered round her with contempt. At first, Janice Woolley and her gang had been hostile, and interrupted with jeers. But Uncle Geoff's story had taken hold of them now. They stood with their silly eyes as round as saucers, and their silly mouths open. Janice was practically *drooling*.... And more kids were stopping playing and gathering on the edge of the crowd all the time.

"And in December," she went on,"which is when it first happened, the hand comes out and prowls round the school like a big thin *spider*. It crawls into the classroom, and crawls round the edge of the room, behind the cupboards, an' when it finds a really nasty fat girl – a really *mean* girl – it runs up her legs an' inside her *knickers*...."

Jane had thought up the knickers bit for herself, and when she said it there were little screams all round, and Janice Woolley nearly fainted.

"But it's December *now*!" said Janice.

"It always happens on the twenty-first of December – that's a week tomorrow."

"Why ain't we heard this story before?" asked Avril Harker suspiciously.

"Because it's only the top class who ever see it," said Jane smugly. "And they never tell anybody – they're too scared to. My Uncle Geoff told me; his son Robert was here when it first happened."

*

Five days later, Jane reported back to Uncle Geoff, entirely satisfied. Janice Woolley and her gang had tried to take the story over; but everyone kept coming back to Jane for further details, which she was now quite good at inventing for herself. The story was all round the school; and the spidery hand had been reported sighted in many places, including even the boys' toilets.

That was the final triumph, if the boys believed it. It had quite swept the ghost of Rosalie Scott from the scene.

"Don't play it up too much, Jane," said Uncle Geoff cautiously. "We don't want people having nightmares."

"It only attacks *nasty* girls," said Jane coolly. She had made quite certain who was having the nightmares.

"But the whole point about it," said Uncle Geoff firmly, "is that it's a *lie*. You helped me make it up, so you *know* it's not true. Just as you now know the rubbish about Rosalie Scott wasn't true. And I want you to remember that all your life. The world is full of great big lies that people want to believe, because they're exciting. That's how ghost-stories start."

Jane felt suddenly bored with Uncle Geoff; she couldn't stand it when grown-ups turned *preachy*.

It was in maths, on the twenty-first of December, that Tracy Merridew screamed. It was about half-past three in the afternoon and raining, nearly dark outside already. The lights were on in the classroom, but they seemed very far away, high up near the ceiling; and the dull planked floor under the tables was full of dusty shadows.

"For *goodness*' sake," shouted Miss Hood, "will you be quiet, Tracy? I am *sick* of this class. I know we break up tomorrow, but today we are *working!*"

But everyone was turning and staring at the dark space beneath the cupboard where the textbooks and the library were kept. The girls were huddling together and the boys were crouching tense, getting ready to be brave. As a whisper went round the room.

"The hand! The hand!"

Then something scuttled with a dry noise, under the cupboard; half-appeared, a dull grey, then vanished again.

"Good God," said Miss Hood. "A mouse. Or a rat!"

As she often told them, she was a farmer's daughter, with no time for nonsense. "We'll soon deal with *that!*" She picked up her heavy blackboard pointer, which she had been known to poke people with, and made straight for the cupboard. She banged on the side of the cupboard with the pointer, making a terrific din. Hoping to scare the rat out.

Nothing stirred.

Very bravely, or very foolishly, she knelt down and peered underneath, her rather large bottom in its loud check skirt humped up in the air. Still peering, she poked the pointer into the darkness, and rattled it about.

Then she gave such a scream as made Tracy Merridew's seem a squeak.

And collapsed in a dead faint.

And as she lay there a thing like a shrivelled hand, but also like a great thin grey spider, seemed to crawl out from under the cupboard and crawl on to her back;

137

crawl up on to her woolly black jumper. Everyone in the class saw it quite clearly, outlined against Miss Hood's black jumper. So all the rest of their lives they would never forget it. . . .

Everyone started screaming.

Then the classroom door burst open, and Mrs Winterbottom was shouting: "What is all this nonsense? Miss Hood. . . . Miss Hood!"

And by the time they had got Miss Hood into her chair and splashed her with water, and tried to tell Mrs Winterbottom what had happened, and turned back to the cupboard, the hand was quite gone.

Jane sat on a hard chair in Mrs Winterbottom's study, and stared out at the night. It was only ten past four, but it was as black as pitch out there. The rest of the school had been sent home; even the top class, after a roasting telling-off from Mrs Winterbottom on the topic of childhood silliness, especially female silliness.

Now Mrs Winterbottom was busy getting to the bottom of it all. At least, she was muttering at regular intervals that she was *going* to get to the bottom of it all, if it *killed* her.

Miss Hood sat in another hard chair, with a strong cup of tea at her elbow. Miss Hood had had three strong cups of tea since she came out of her faint, but she was still very pale and a bit sweaty, as if she'd just got up in the morning.

Jane had told her story, in between outbursts of tears. Uncle Geoff had been summoned by telephone. She was cheered when the lights of his big old black Daimler turned in at the school gates.

He came in looking very excited, but also a bit shifty, like a boy who's been caught scrumping apples. He sat and listened patiently, while Mrs Winterbottom did her nut about his extremely irresponsible behaviour. When she had finally finished, he turned briskly to Miss Hood and said: "And what exactly *did* you see, Miss Hood?"

Miss Hood was silent a long time, as if the future of the human race depended upon her answer. Then she said reluctantly: "It looked like a shrivelled hand. And it moved . . . sort of *crawled*." She turned even paler, and Jane thought she was going to faint again.

"And what were you *expecting* to see, Miss Hood?" Uncle Geoff had gone extra-gentle.

"A rat, of course. I was going to kill it. I've often killed them on my father's farm."

"So," said Uncle Geoff, "Miss Hood was expecting a rat. She was quite brave, because she is used to killing rats. And instead she saw a human hand. You can hardly blame that on me – or on female hysteria, Mrs Winterbottom. Miss Hood, had you heard any whisper of my story about the hand?"

"No. After Tracy screamed, the children kept saying to each other 'the hand, the hand'. But I didn't know what they were talking about. . . ."

"What did *you* see, when you opened the classroom door, Mrs Winterbottom?" Uncle Geoff's eyes were suddenly as fierce and keen as the Head's.

Finally, Mrs Winterbottom said reluctantly: "The light was poor. There was something grey on Miss Hood's jumper. It definitely wasn't a mouse or a rat."

There was a long silence, with only the heavy tick of

the old schoolroom clock on the wall. A clock as old as the school itself. Then Mrs Winterbottom said: "There are *tropical* spiders that size. . . ."

"But it's hardly tropical weather, Mrs Winterbottom, is it?"

"I've read about them coming over in crates of tropical fruit. . . ."

"How many crates of tropical fruit do you see in this school?"

"Children can do incredible things . . . a boy could have smuggled it in. . . ."

"Without any of the other children spotting him? I would like to believe that. But I don't. And neither do you."

There was something terrible for Jane in Mrs Winterbottom's weary gesture of defeat. She continued feebly, "It will be all over the village by now. What am I to tell the parents? What am I to tell County Hall?"

Another long silence. Then Uncle Geoff said gently: "D'you mind if I have another look at that stock room?"

"You surely don't believe . . . "

"I don't know *what* I believe, Mrs Winterbottom."

Mrs Winterbottom said, with a sudden desperate spurt of her old spirit: "I shall certainly come with you. . . ."

"I'll come, too," said Miss Hood, with a nervous glance at the rather large gap beneath the Head's study door.

"Please don't leave me," said Jane.

Again they climbed the concrete stairs. Uncle Geoff

leading, Mrs Winterbottom and Jane in hot pursuit and Miss Hood bringing up the rear, glancing nervously behind her every few steps.

The papier-mâché masks leered down; still stirred in the draught that came through the roof-slates, like a boy trying to whistle between his teeth.

"What's behind that door?" asked Uncle Geoff, pointing at the door at the back, the door with no name on it, not even in yellow cracked paint.

"I don't know," said the Head. "The roof-space, I suppose. The main roof over the classrooms. . . ." Jane had never heard her sound less bossy.

Uncle Geoff leant forward to pull it open; gingerly, as if the handle might have been red-hot. Jane wanted to scream: "Don't, Uncle Geoff, don't!" She had an awful vision of Rosalie Scott floating out like in her dreams, flat as a penny sideways, flat as a floppy photograph. . . .

But there was only darkness and silence, with the faint sound of a boy whistling.

Uncle Geoff shut the door a lot quicker than he'd opened it. Then he said, talking as if to the air, with shocking gentleness: "Rosalie, are you there? Rosalie, we want to help."

The scenic backdrop, with the trees like lollipops, fell down off the wall with a crash; then sagged slowly against Uncle Geoff, like a wall toppling, or a great chimney falling. Uncle Geoff staggered, then pushed the backdrop against the wall.

"Why did it do that?" said the Head, sounding furiously angry. "No one touched it. . . ."

"Rosalie, are you there?" asked Uncle Geoff again. "Rosalie, we do want to help...." His voice was so sad.

A bundle of old hockey-sticks rattled suddenly in the corner, like dry bones.

"Who did that?" shouted the Head. "Who's up here playing tricks? Come out or I'll...."

The cheap golden crown rose slowly from the broken golden throne all on its own and then hit Uncle Geoff a sharp blow on the face, then fell to the floor with a tinny sound and rolled away into a corner. Uncle Geoff put his hand up to his face, and Jane watched a thin trickle of blood come out between his fingers. Suddenly, the way he was standing, he no longer looked like her great wizard, but like a frail old man.

And suddenly Jane was furious. He was *her* Uncle Geoff. And Rosalie Scott was being as spiteful as Janice Woolley. She ran forward and put her arm round her uncle; and shouted to the air: "Leave him alone, you stupid cow. He's only trying to help you!"

But once she'd started she found she couldn't stop. Her voice went on and on of itself.

"Oh, you've had a lovely time all these years, frightening little kids! Hiding away up here. Because you were scared to go to the big school! Scaredy-cat! Scaredy-cat! Well, you've done it now, haven't you? The teachers know about you properly now. Now they'll have to do something about you. You won't be allowed to stay here any more. Now you'll *have* to go to the big school." Jane knew she was being horribly spiteful, but she was horribly scared.

142

And suddenly all the stuff in that jumbled room was in motion. Papier-mâché masks and chairs and shepherds' crooks from the Nativity Play were battering at them like angry birds. They backed away to the door in a bunch, holding their hands in front of their faces.

But in the dark corridor the old tennis-rackets and shrunken netballs were pummelling them. And in the staff room the kettle went straight for Miss Hood's head, then bounced off her defending hand and fell to the carpet, spilling its contents in a great dark jet.

Somehow they got downstairs and into the Head's study and Uncle Geoff slammed the door and shot the bolt.

"Ring for the police, Mrs Winterbottom," pleaded Miss Hood.

"And what shall I *say* to them, Miss Hood?" shouted the Head with a touch of her old asperity.

"Listen," whispered Miss Hood. "In the classrooms. The desks are moving. . . ."

They listened with great shuddering breaths to the desks being dragged about.

"Cleaners?" asked Uncle Geoff.

"Not until five o'clock," said Mrs Winterbottom. "They do the infants' school till then."

Uncle Geoff looked at his watch. Jane could see it was only half-past four.

"I suggest," he said, "we discuss this further *outside*."

It was to their credit that they didn't run.

*

They all sat in Uncle Geoffrey's car, huddled together for safety, and watched the school. The lights were still on in the Head's study downstairs, and in the staff room upstairs, but the rest of the school was in darkness. And they could still hear the desks being thrown about.

"It's so . . . hateful . . . and violent," said Miss Hood in a trembling voice. "It's the *hate* I can't stand . . . I didn't know children could *hate* like that."

Oh, Miss Hood, thought Jane, how little you know.

"Children hate," said Uncle Geoffrey, "but they also like rules and law and order. I'm afraid there are no rules where Rosalie Scott is now."

"There's just nobody I can *ring*," said the Head hopelessly. "But I know one thing. I will allow no child of mine back in that place until the whole thing is cleared up. And I don't mind if County do ask for my resignation. . . ." Having made up her mind, she sounded a bit better.

"There was always a funny feeling in that stock room," said Miss Hood. "A cold miserable feeling. I never liked going there myself. But you can't let feelings get in the way of your work."

"What's *that*?" asked Uncle Geoffrey, making them all jump.

Something was happening to the roof, just about where the stock room should be. The cracks between the slates were outlined in a flickering blue light; it came and went in bursts.

"It looks electrical to me," said Uncle Geoffrey. "A short circuit in your wiring. All that stuff being thrown about – how old is your electric wiring?"

"Too old," said the Head, "like the rest of the school. They've done no maintenance for years, with the financial cuts. They keep on promising to build us a new school – ICI want this land back for an alkali-store. But they keep on putting off starting the new building. This one's over a hundred years old...."

What happened next happened so swiftly that they could only sit and watch as if paralysed. The light of the staff-room window turned a subtle red, and began to flicker. Then steam seemed to be coming through all the cracks between the slates in the roof, thin, white, ghostly. It was all so unreal that they just sat and watched. Then the roof above the stock room seemed to sag, crack apart, and the next second red flames and showers of sparks were roaring into the night sky, just like they had for the big town bonfire on November the Fifth.

"The whole roof's on fire," said Uncle Geoffrey.

"I must ring the fire brigade," said the Head. She seemed almost happy, knowing who to ring up at last.

"It won't do any good," said Uncle Geoff. "It's got too big a hold. I think you're going to get your new school sooner than you think, Mrs Winterbottom ..."

"On a different site, thank God."

"Oh, all my teaching aids," said Miss Hood. "And the children's projects.... Is there time to save them?"

"I forbid you to go in there, Miss Hood," said the Head briskly. And they all went on sitting there, it seemed to Jane increasingly cheerfully, almost as if

Journey

Ted wakened in blackness.

And total silence.

He tried to shout. Nothing came. Not even a whimper.

He felt for his mouth, to see why it didn't work.

No mouth, no hands, no body at all. Only the memory of having had body, mouth, hands.

Terror filled him like ice. He started to scream. And couldn't. He realized for the first time what a privilege it had been to scream, whimper, hide his face in his hands. He couldn't do any of it.

It's a dream ... a nightmare.

No dream had ever been as bad as this. And he'd always been able to wake himself out of nightmares; but he couldn't wake out of this. It just went on and on and on. He wished he could faint; but he couldn't.

How the hell had he got into this state? Had someone slipped LSD into his drink?

He remembered going to the Blue Dolphin on his bike for a fish-and-chip supper. Arguing with Togger Tawse about the Isle of Man TT races. Togger reckoned the BMWs would wipe the Nips off the face of the earth in the big bike race this year. That was the last thing he remembered doing. No harm in arguing. He was always arguing.

But slowly another memory came creeping in, unwelcome as long strands of midnight mist creeping across the road into the beam of your headlight.

He'd set out for home...doing seventy up the Marton Road....

That car, waiting at the end of Appleby Street... waiting to turn right, across his front. A funny indecisive car that kept edging forward nervously, as if it couldn't make up its mind....

Suddenly, he'd felt a spurt of irrational rage: *I'll make up your mind for you, you bastard.* And turned on the juice....

At the same moment the bloody stupid car had begun to cross in front of him. He'd clapped the anchors on, knowing it was too late. Steered the bike behind the car, as it swung across him. No point steering in front....

A tremendous thump, without pain, and he was flying, flying through the dark, way up into the sky like a rocket, like a dreamy bird. Then another thump.

Then nothing. Till this.

I must be dead, he thought. Dead, dead, dead. The word rolled round his mind like the beating of a drum.

Oddly, it calmed him. At least he knew where he was. He always liked to know where he was. Must just be a matter of waiting now. *They* must know that he was dead, since They were supposed to know everything. They'd send somebody along to collect him in a minute. They wouldn't just leave people floating about in nothing; that was untidy. And, if he was convinced of nothing else, he was convinced They would be tidy. After all, They had the Universe to run. They couldn't afford to be untidy, or you'd get planets colliding. . . . He wondered what They'd send to collect him. Not an angel off a Christmas card. . . . What a giggle, to be picked up by a plastic glitter angel. He would have giggled if he could. He felt better.

Better enough to take stock of himself. He felt like a bubble – a bubble full of feelings and memories, just floating. But he discovered that, if he thought hard enough, he could sort of *move*; like those wriggling amoebas he'd once seen under the microscope in the biol lab at school.

But he soon tired of wriggling; it exhausted his mind, and he was feeling pretty knackered anyway. And since there was nowhere to move to there didn't seem much point. He wished They'd come and collect him, PDQ.

He waited. Nothing happened. Maybe They weren't so efficient after all? Maybe They only came round once a week, if you were lucky, like the dustmen at home? Sometimes *they* didn't come for three weeks at a time. Oh, shit, shit, *shit*. If They left him that long, he'd go potty like some head-banger in solitary. . . .

And then, in the middle of a new flurry of rising panic, he sensed he wasn't alone any more. He could hear nothing, see nothing, feel nothing. Yet somehow he knew there was another bubble creeping up behind him, wriggling slowly towards him. Not a very nice bubble – bubble set on . . . eating him.

He found he could wriggle faster than he thought – a

149

very long desperate wriggle, which he thought would never end. But at last he sensed the other bubble tire, despair, and go drifting away after other prey.

After that, he stayed alert, sending out his mind wider and wider. Now he could sense other bubbles floating round him in the dark. All were sad, lost. Some were drifting in a daze. He felt one give a flash of terror as something ate it. He worked very hard at keeping himself to himself now, remembering ruefully the time he had thought he was alone.

Until the big bubble came straight for him. It wanted him *very* badly. It wanted him with all its heart. So, slowly, slowly, it gained on him.

He kept going as long as he could.

And in the end gave up.

But the big bubble didn't eat him. It floated alongside, diffidently. He began picking up its thoughts.

Teeth, biting, chewing.... He tried to sidle away again. But the thing followed.

Then he got the memory of a well-chewed ball. A blue and yellow ball. Lying on badly mown grass. Then a hand with black hairs on the back reached down for the ball; a glimpse of a laughing face with a moustache – a policeman in blue shirt-sleeves. And voices – a man's voice, a woman's, a child's calling "Zero, Zero, Zero!" Suddenly he knew that the other bubble had been an Alsatian bitch, a police-dog called Zero.

He was so relieved he opened his mind and let her in. A police-dog seemed a very good thing to have in a place like this.

He was deluged with a tornado of joy. It felt as if the

dog had leapt into his arms and was licking his face all over. Still the voices called "Zero, Zero!"

But all Zero's love was now for him. She had suffered so much blackness and loneliness it made Ted shudder.

He'd been nervous, all the time that Zero was going crazy over him, that something big and nasty would creep up and swallow them both. But now they were settled he realized he had rather less to fear in that direction. Not only was their combined bubble bigger; several nasty bubbles cleared off abruptly when they felt Zero's protective rage.

It made Ted bold; it also gave him a purpose in life. Together, they would go and look for more *nice* lonely bubbles, and join them, and get bigger and stronger still. He set off with a certain weird swagger. Zero, dog-like, took it as going for a walk and was delighted.

But the search proved harder than he thought. Many bubbles sheered away from his very size and determination; some became absolutely terrified, so although Ted could've overtaken them he hadn't the heart. But he managed to pick up another big simple bubble that turned out to be a grieving golden Labrador called Cindy, and a smaller one that had been a Jack Russell terrier called Jim. There was much canine excitement. Ted felt rather left out. Still, he was glad to get Jim aboard; Jim, in spite of his doughty courage, had been nearly eaten many times, and it was a long time before his terror subsided.

There must be a lot more dogs to rescue. They set off again. And now it seemed as if dog called to dog. They were coming in thick and fast; a border collie, a Great

Dane pup, a spoilt and elderly poodle. . . . A pack was forming. Sometimes they had to stop for a long time, in a whirl of confusion, while the pack-order was sorted out. But always Zero remained on top, a merciful and motherly leader, a typical bitch.

The pack drove on through the dark with a life of its own. Ted was content to be pulled along. He now felt inside a long black bubble, sort of sausage-shaped, that was really going somewhere, even though he'd no idea where.

And then something grabbed them; something really huge. There was a moment of heaving and straining, and then it had swallowed them whole.

And it seemed to Ted he was in a room: a grey room that stank sweetly of old people; a room with tall dark Victorian mirrors and worn armchairs, in which a couple sat. The old man's thin hand picked compulsively at the arm of his chair; it looked like a bird that was busy pecking into the chair. Pieces of stuffing kept coming out, and the thin hand rolled them into balls, then threw them down on the threadbare carpet. The man was bald, his bald head mottled with brown liver-spots. By his feet, panting, sat a wretched old spaniel.

But, if the old man was appalling, the old woman was worse. Her flesh hung like draped curtains across the sharp edges of her bones; only her eyes were alive and hungry, and filled with seeping hate.

"Our daughter," she said. "We are looking for our daughter. They have taken her away." But her eyes measured Ted speculatively.

"Sod off," said Ted, returning her hate with interest. And, at his words, every dog threw itself upon her. She vanished under a mass of writing, snarling dog-bodies....

There was a sort of explosion; and then Ted found himself back in the darkness of his own bubble, with the dogs writhing around like crazy, sorting themselves out. When peace returned, Ted could still sense the other bubble following. But it seemed to him a little smaller now, and his own a little bigger. Then the other bubble gave up, and went limpingly away.

It was only then that he realized they had another dog on board: the couple's sad old spaniel, a terror-paralysed spaniel called Dick....

They had taken him away from the dreadful couple. Slowly Dick was coming back to life. Slowly, thought Ted, the spaniel was finding death worth living. He giggled in his mind, then took hold of himself firmly.

The pack forged on, still seeking dogs. Ted wondered vaguely how many dogs he could take. But he wasn't really worried. Zero was boss, and Zero was his. Every so often her warm stern maternal presence touched him in the darkness, reassuringly. Why did dogs have this need to serve man? But just as well....

The plea for help shot through the bubble like a knife. The pleading was human, female.

"Oh, no, no, no, noooooh." Each "no" was like a desperate fist, beating helplessly against a second worse dying; like a sicking-up of a fact too horrible to stay in the mind.

Ted didn't hesitate a second. He was against people being eaten, and was swollen with the pride and strength of his pack.

"Go, Zero, go!"

The pack surged forward; they, too, were full of the pride and strength of being a pack. Ted sensed their gathering speed.

It must have been the pride and speed that did it. Ted sensed the utter amazement of the Eater as they hit it. It was used to having all its own way in this part of the dark. That was what saved them. For as they hit it Ted realized it was something so huge, so merciless and so evil that it made a great white shark seem like a minnow by comparison.

There was a sense of endless teeth, and a red rage of appetite, and then they had bounced off it again. Then the Eater was getting over its surprise, and turning, coming back to eat them. And Ted knew it was far too big to cope with. They *were* going to be eaten. . . .

Then there was a new wave of thought, inside the bubble with them. A sort of incoherent silent gabbling. . . .

"Our Father, which art in Heaven . . . Holy Mary, Mother of God. . . ."

The Eater checked uncertainly, hovering. The torrent of incoherent prayer went on and on and on, and somehow Ted sensed the Eater *disliked* it, as you might dislike a nail sticking up in your shoe. The Eater surveyed them a long time, without hurry and without mercy. As Ted might have contemplated a congealing hamburger. While the torrent of jumbled prayer went on and on and on.

Then the Eater turned away in disgust. Leaving them like a cold sausage on a greasy plate.

"You can stop now," ordered Ted to the endless stream of prayers. "It's gone." Then, thoughtfully, to Zero: "Get some more dogs."

The stream of prayers turned into terrified grief, which slowly abated. But they had acquired seven more dogs before the timid human thought came.

"Where am I?"

"I don't know. I think we're dead. My name's Ted. You're safe now – sort of safe anyway. What's your name?"

"Maureen Kelly. I'm a nurse at Cresham General. I don't know what's happened."

"What's the last thing you remember?"

"I was at a disco – no I was walking home, on my own, because I'd had a row with Trevor. . . . I was just passing those allotments on Southam Street when somebody . . . grabbed me. . . ." This time the storm of grief and agony was so great that Ted felt the balloon of darkness must burst into a thousand fragments. The dogs were stilled, inert, cringing and cowering, they were just drifting, open to any Eater. . . .

The unbearable storm ceased in the end.

The timid thought came again: "How did you . . . die?"

"Crashed me bike. . . ."

"Are we really dead? I keep thinking it's a dream, and if I open my eyes. . . ."

"It's not; and you can't."

"What can we do? If we could only *see*!"

"You can sort of *feel*. Try feeling outwards with your mind. Can you feel all the dogs round us?"

"So what are we *supposed* to do?"

"I think . . . we have to find our own way to wherever it is. But I can't tell which direction it is, so there seems no real point in going anywhere. All I know is that there's things out there that eat you, and there's safety in numbers. So I'm picking up everything I can. An' your prayers seemed to work an' all. They really sickened that Eater...."

"You can't use prayer like a machine-gun...." She sounded very shocked. Ted thought she must be a Catholic.

"If it works, use it. That's my bloody motto. D'you want to be eaten? If I say pray, you bloody *pray*, right?"

"I suppose so." She still felt doubtful, but a lot brisker, more nurselike. "What do we do next, then?"

"Try to rescue some more people, I suppose."

"Like you ... rescued me?"

"Sort of." Ted felt suddenly awkward. There was a gratitude in her thought that embarrassed him. How odd, he thought. I'm dead, but I can still be embarrassed.

"Let's go and rescue something," he said abruptly.

"There's a lot of cats out there. But they're sheering off – I think they're frightened of your dogs. And some little things I think are horses."

"I thought horses would've been *big*."

"No – they've got very small minds. A bit stupid. But they're getting together in clusters, so I think they'll be all right."

"You can sense a lot more than me – you're like bloody radar."

"I don't think you ought to swear so much. You don't know who's listening."

"You mean the holy angels might be watching over us?"

"Please don't mock."

"The holy angels didn't do much for you when you were being eaten...."

"Are you an atheist?"

"Doesn't seem much point to that, now I'm dead."

"There's someone up ahead, I think."

"I can't feel anything."

"Of course not. Men are always less sensitive."

"I'm getting it now."

It would have been impossible not to. It was a storm of woe much worse even than she had put up; a beacon of ceaseless silent wailing. As they grew near, it grew as painful as walking into a fire. Even Zero began to falter.

"Look, I think we'd better steer clear of this ... it's too much for us ... it'll wreck us. The dogs are panicking ... we won't be able to keep off the Eaters...."

"*You* can do what you like. *I'm* going to him. Run along and save your rotten little soul." And in a second she'd slipped away. Ted sensed her moving nearer and nearer to that terrible wailing.

He dithered, anxiously. He could sense the wailing sapping the energy of the dogs – but if he left her an Eater would certainly get her.

He made up his mind; took the dogs out to a bearable distance. Then, as their courage returned, he drove them round and round in a huge circle, covering her as best he could, thinking as fierce thoughts as possible to frighten off the Eaters. The pack, in sympathy, set up a silent baying like a hunting pack, all of one mind after some quarry unknown.

He seemed to circle for ever, but no big Eaters came. He sensed smaller nasty stuff sheering away from them, which felt great. But at the same time more and more dogs kept coming in, drawn by the excitement of the chase.

At last there was a heavenly stillness; the old man with Maureen had fallen silent. Her thought came through the dark, clear as a bell.

"You can come now; I've got him settled."

"Thanks, Nurse!"

"Sister, to you!"

"By, that's a terrible lot of dogs, hinny." The old man's thought was weak and thankful and quavery.

"There's somebody else over there!"

"God, can't we take a break? I'm dizzy with running in circles."

"There's an Eater after her!"

That was more like it. He urged the pack into the attack, with all the power of his mind. How big the pack was now! How powerful! But he still asked her to pray....

"Look, prayer's not magic ... not a *weapon*."

"Bless the dogs, then. That can't do any harm."

"I'll recite a psalm if you like."

"One of the warlike ones, then. *Not* the twenty-third. . . ."

He was wild with the hunt now, wilder than the dogs. He could sense the Eater; it was big, but it was growing uneasy, and starting to flinch to one side. In a minute, it would be running and they would be after it. The pack would tear it to bits. . . .

The Eater *was* running now; it seemed to be shrinking smaller from very terror. Shrinking to a mouthful for Zero, who was in the lead. . . .

"*Stop!*" Maureen's voice was so forceful that the pack stopped dead, and dissolved into total bafflement and confusion.

"What the hell did you do that for?" Ted was beside himself with rage. "We nearly had the bastard."

"You were ... turning into an Eater yourself ... and, if you'd eaten it, it would've become *part* of us ... and you'd have wanted to go on eating more and more...."

"God...." He was quiet a long time. "D'you really think *that*?"

"Like on earth," she added briskly, nurselike. "You are what you eat.... Now, the person we've come to save is *here*."

And, indeed, there was a querulous elderly female thought, going on and on and on. "What do *you* want? What *do* you think you're doing? I'm trying to get a little rest. How can I, with all this disturbance? All I want is a little peace and quiet ... a little *privacy*."

Oh God, thought Ted, she's one of *those* ... one of those old bags who're always complaining when I rev my bike.

"I'll talk to her." He felt Maureen slip away.

The old man asked anxiously: "That little lady's coming back, isn't she, sir?"

"Oh, yes, she'll be back. She won't get far wi' this one."

It was peaceful. The dogs went back to their endless activity of sorting each other out. There was a big Dobe, who tried coming it with Zero; but she soon put him in his place. Ted tuned in idly to the old woman's thoughts.

"I'm sorry, young woman. I'm sure you mean well,

but I am not traipsing about with a pack of dogs. . . ." Then a little later: "That will be *quite* enough. I think you forget I'm old enough to be your mother. I am entitled to a little respect. I do not like dogs, I do not like scruffy old men, and I certainly do not like that young motorbike yob you've got involved with. I have led a respectable life, keeping myself to myself and bothering nobody. . . ."

To his surprise, Ted felt Maureen slip back aboard. "You've given up quick. . . ."

"Yes." Maureen seemed so faint and exhausted that Ted felt a sudden fear for her. But he was also appalled.

"If we leave her, an Eater will get her. . . ."

"I think it's inevitable. I almost feel sorry for the Eater. I think the Eaters are made up of people like her – people who *hate*. Just like we're made up of things that love."

"Me – love?" Ted was embarrassed again.

"Oh, you're not very good at it. But you did care about the dogs, didn't you? And me?"

"Suppose so. . . ."

"So let's get moving. We could do with a bit of help. I think there's some up ahead."

Ted urged the dogs forward. He didn't have to ask in what direction. The thing up ahead was as strong as a beacon. A tiny sun of hope? Warmth?

So he was surprised at the thoughts that came from it; it made him want to giggle. Another old lady.

"I will cling to the Old Rugged Cross
And exchange it some day for a crown. . . ."

There was a ring of Eaters circling round her, but they seemed pretty discouraged, like a pack of unsuccessful jackals.

The old lady nipped aboard immediately.

"Hello, hinnies. By, you got here quick! I'm not halfway through me repertoire."

"Don't stop singing, Gran!" thought Ted. She seemed to make the whole balloon of darkness warmer, as if someone had started up a central-heating system.

"Mind who ye're calling Gran, me bonnie-lad. Mrs Sarah Teasdale's me title, and none of your lip. By, ye've got a strong pack o' dogs wi'ye. Ah thowt Ah wes goin' to Heaven, but it looks like we're goin' to the Dogs' Home first."

"Do you know which way . . . Heaven . . . is supposed to be, Mrs Teasdale?"

"Not a clue, hinny. Ah thowt ye'd come to fetch *me*. There doesn't seem nobody to ask, does there? Still, we're aal in the Lord's hand. Aah've been wi' the Army aal me life. . . ."

Ted couldn't help teasing her. "The British Army, Mrs Teasdale?"

"Gerraway, ye cheeky young pup! Teasing an old woman. The Sally Army o' course. Ah'm a Salvationist." She continued her hymns where she'd left off. She seemed to know an endless number; they sprang from her like a continuous roll of holy toilet paper. But Ted was glad of them; he hadn't realized how cold he'd felt till now. The dogs liked it. The old man began to sing along with her haltingly. Maureen joined in, and even Ted hummed along, though he didn't know any of the words.

But which way now? Indeed, there was no one to ask.

161

The darkness was empty, even of Eaters. Only one solitary bull terrier coming in as fast as a comet in its eagerness. He searched the blackness, further and further out, to the limits of his mind. Nothing now.

But the pack was restless to be on the move again. They seemed happier when they were on the move.

His mind searched on endlessly. And then it seemed to him the darkness on the right was a little less dark than the blackness on the left. The difference between black and very, very dark grey.

Well, he was all for the light.

They sped into the dark, dark greyness. It seemed to him, after a long, long while that it grew a little lighter still.

"Ah think ye're heading the wrong way, bonnie-lad."

He abruptly pulled the dogs into a scrambling, writhing halt. A terrible rage seized him. He'd made up his mind with *enormous* difficulty when nobody was willing to help, and now she was muddling him up. God, this never-ending dark. He was so *sick* of it. His rage nearly blew the balloon apart; the dogs went into hysterics again.

"Steady, Ted." Maureen's gentle thought touched him like a warm hand, comforting. "We know it's hard. Try to keep your cool."

He pulled himself together with an effort, and asked politely: "Why do you think that, Mrs Teasdale?"

"Ah divvent knaa, hinny. I just feel Aah've done this bit before. It feels the wrong way, somehow."

"Ye're right there, missus," quavered the old man. "Ah wes havin' the same thowt meself...."

"You want me to head into the *dark*?" Then, a little

more calmly: "What do you think, Maureen?"

Maureen was a long time turning things over in her mind. Finally she said: "I don't know, Ted. Both ways seem the same to me."

"You're a fat lot of help. Well, we've got all the time there is. And the dogs don't seem to get tired. Let's try a bit more of my way first; then, if it doesn't work, we'll try your way, Mrs Teasdale."

"Ah'm content, hinny. We're aal in the Lord's hand." She fell to singing again; the old man sang with her; they were getting very close.

They seemed to go on for ever. But travelling in one direction made Ted content; gave him the illusion they were actually getting somewhere. And all the time the light grew a little stronger. But it showed up nothing. It became like a dense fog, with the sun shining through it, stronger and stronger.

And then . . . no . . . yes . . . what looked like the outline of a great pyramid, a pyramid so vast that Ted gasped. Then another, then another.

"Look, Maureen, look, *look*! I can see. We got there, we got there." He was babbling with joy.

"Look. The fog's coloured. All blue and pink." Maureen's delight was as drunken as his own.

But Mrs Teasdale said sadly: "Ye've come to the wrong place, hinny. Ah'm certain of it now."

"I don't care. We're *somewhere*. I can *see*!"

Then he turned to look at Maureen, to see what she was like.

He couldn't see her at all. He couldn't see Mrs Teasdale or the old man or the dogs, either. He couldn't see any part of himself. It was as if he was a single eye alone, tearing through a landscape of coloured mist and dim pyramids.

Desperately he tried to force the dogs to go lower, nearer. Like a 747 coming in to land. But for some reason they wouldn't go any lower; they just skimmed on, very fast.

"Ye're goin' to be disappointed, hinny," said Mrs Teasdale sadly.

Enraged, he turned the full fury of his will on the dogs. Like a whip. They whimpered and writhed. But still they refused to go lower.

And then they stopped suddenly, as if they'd hit a brick wall. And nothing Ted could do would make them move again. They were still there, quite peaceful; but beyond any power of his.

There was something ahead, hidden by the mist.

He knew by the feel of it that it wasn't an Eater. Or a dog or a cat or a horse or a human.

"What the hell are you?" he screamed at it with his mind. "What the hell do you want?"

No answer.

"Get out of the way – you're scaring the dogs!"

But it came to Ted that it had been *him* that had been scaring the dogs. The thing ahead had rendered the dogs perfectly calm.

"I suppose you're some sort of bloody angel? Where were you when we needed you? When the Eaters were eating people? You scared of them or something? Is this the best you can do, stopping people from getting where they want, when they've got there under their own steam?"

There was no answer. But the thing was real; far realler than any Eater; far realler than Ted; as real as the surface of the road when you hit it with your face. . . .

"If you think I'm going back *there*, into the dark, where they eat people, you must be out of your tiny shiny—"

"Ted!" The thought came urgently from Maureen. "One of the saints said that in God is a deep but glittering darkness. . . ."

"I don't want your Catholic rubbish – I want the *light*!"

"Ah've got no choice, hinny." It was Mrs Teasdale. "Ah'm dead and Ah know it. And so is this old feller, and aal the dogs but one. Dead and their poor little bodies burnt already. . . ."

An awful choking smothering despair descended on Ted. "But I don't *feel* dead!"

"Neither do I, Ted." The comforting thought came from Maureen. "I want to go on living. I've got things to do. . . ."

"Ah think you two have the choice, hinnies. To go on, or go back. That's why we're stuck here. . . ."

"Only, sir," quavered the old man very respectfully, "if you're going back, could you do me a great favour? It's me dog, sir. He's in Potherton Dogs' Home. A fox terrier called Budger, wi' a black spot on the side of his nose. Ah divvent want them to put him to sleep, just cos Ah'm dead. He's still a young dog, see?"

Ted reassured him. But after all that had happened he felt no trust in the powers that ruled the universe any more. No trust in anything but himself. "Maureen, if we choose to go back, what kind of bodies are we going back *to*? I've known some bikers who survived – in wheelchairs. All they could do was make funny noises and drool. Like cabbages. This bastard in front might let us go back and then we'd find ourselves like *that*."

He felt the same trembling doubt in Maureen, who'd seen even worse cases. Then he felt her remember her mum and dad, and nursing. "It's a risk we've got to take, Ted!"

And then she was gone. And Mrs Teasdale and the old man and all the dogs were gone. And the mist was drifting away from the tall pyramids, and they became the icy fangs of enormous mountains, cracking in bitter frost. He heard the grinding rumble of glaciers, and felt the howling wind that cut like a knife. He felt all the cruelty of the world, which matched the cruelty of the dark where things got eaten. He knew he had to choose between the two cruelties, and he couldn't.

Then he remembered the utter solidness of the angel-thing, with whom it was pointless to argue. If he made it through the dark, he would only come to a place where they were all like that; where you'd never be able to argue again. And not being able to argue made life not worth living; if you couldn't argue, then you were worse than dead. You were a lap-dog, God's poodle. . . .

He hoped the dogs would keep Mrs Teasdale safe – or would Mrs Teasdale keep the dogs safe? In the muddly dark, no way of knowing. . . .

He chose.

Christ, the pain! He'd never known such pain. He opened his eyes to see what was hurting him.

A high white ceiling, a long rectangular light-fitting, and a smell that said hospital.

He swung his head from one side to the other. Saw

fat polythene bags of liquid hanging over him, like transparent pigs hanging in a butcher's shop; thin pipes looping down towards him.

Then a large warm hand grabbed his, and he heard his father say: "Tell Sister he's coming round."

His eyes found his father's face. His father looked like an old tramp, with a grey, lined, saggy face, and two days' growth of whiskers, and greasy strands of hair hanging down over the collar of a very dirty shirt. Was his hair *really* that grey?

He tried to squeeze his father's hand; his own hand felt ridiculous and puny like it was made of elastic bands. He looked at it, craning his neck. His fingers looked thin and white and horribly clean, where they lay in his father's.

Some nurse bustled in, read various dials as briskly as a U-boat commander about to dive, and told Dad to wait outside in the corridor.

Dad rose to go, stretching his legs one by one like a very old man. He picked up a paper that was lying on the bed. Trust Dad to get a bit of reading in, no matter what. . . .

Then the big print of the headline swam into focus: "POLICE DOG ZERO FIGHTS FOR LIFE."

"So it wasn't all a dream," said Ted.

"What wasn't?" asked the nurse, still bustling round and not really listening.

"I met a police-dog called Zero. Only I thought it was a dream."

"You must have heard us talking about her, while we thought you were unconscious. Everybody's talking about Zero. She saved a child from being murdered. The man shot her. . . ."

He wasn't prepared to let it pass without an

argument. "What hospital's this?"

"Cresham General, of course. Now, be *quiet*!"

Excitement pounded through his weakened body like an engulfing tidal wave.

"You gotta nurse here called Maureen Kelly? I met her, too. She was attacked...."

The nurse froze. Her fingers tightened round the plastic tube she was adjusting till the knuckles went white and Ted was afraid his lifeline would be cut off.

"I wish," she said at last, "that people wouldn't chatter so in Intensive Care. Patients may *seem* to be unconscious, but they hear far more than anyone thinks. I suppose you heard she was raped and left for dead?"

"She's going to make it – I *know*!"

"Considering she came out of her coma yesterday morning, that's hardly *news*. Now, shut up, or you'll have to have a jab to shut you up, and then your father won't be allowed back...."

He lay back and shut up. This was *terrible*. Was all he'd been through really just a dream that he'd made up of bits of things he'd overheard?

"I'll let your father back in now," said the nurse, softening a bit. "Till Doctor comes...."

Dad came back, with Mum this time, and they both looked terrible, like they should be in Intensive Care themselves. They sat on either side of the bed, and held his hands like they were the Crown Jewels. Dad asked Ted if he could wriggle his toes; which he did, though the nurse gave them all a warning look....

Mum said: "I wish there was something we could do . . . to make things easier, Ted. *Anything!*"

Ted made a weak attempt to laugh, and stopped abruptly as fresh pains hit him. Because there was something she could do. Everyone might have been talking about Zero and Maureen Kelly. But no one would have been talking about a fox terrier called Budger.

"Look, I want you to go to Potherton Dogs' Home...."

Afterwards, he fell back into a warmer, kinder dark.

Knowing he would *know*.